# Classic
# Sportives
## South West England

## ABOUT THE AUTHOR

Colin Dennis has been riding bikes of one sort or another for longer than he dares to remember. His passion for road and off-road cycling has taken him all over the UK and continental Europe, both leading expeditions and for personal pleasure. Plotting, planning and escaping to new locations are pastimes that have driven him for many years, and working as both freelance copywriter and cycle guide provides a happy balance at home and work. Colin is never happier than when he's struggling up a steep climb behind a group, usually covered in mud, but as long as there's a warm tea shop involved – everything's possible. Legs were massaged (but still not shaved) in the making of this guidebook!

# 20
# Classic Sportives
## South West England

by Colin Dennis

2 POLICE SQUARE, MILNTHORPE, CUMBRIA LA7 7PY
www.cicerone.co.uk

First edition 2015

ISBN: 978 1 85284 744 9

Printed in China on behalf of Latitude Press Ltd

A catalogue record for this book is available from the British Library.

All photographs © Colin Dennis except the cover photo © Tony Dymott.

Mapping produced by Lovell Johns Ltd

*This book is dedicated to the memory of my dad – a true man of the south west.*

## Acknowledgements

I would like to thank all my family for their help, support and bars of dark chocolate over the past year. I am also very grateful to Andy Wigmore of Saddleback for the loan of the bike just when I needed one – 'cometh the hour, cometh the man', as they say. For his help over the cobbles of Gold Hill, a big thank you must go out to one of the true gentlemen of the UK's racing scene: the tireless Paul Hopkins. Finally, for his time and professionalism with the cover photo, I am indebted to Tony Dymott of AD Photography, Bournemouth.

## Updates to this Guide

While every effort is made by our authors to ensure the accuracy of guidebooks as they go to print, changes can occur during the lifetime of an edition. Any updates that we know of for this guide will be on the Cicerone website (www.cicerone.co.uk/744/updates), so please check before planning your trip. We also advise that you check information about such things as transport, accommodation and shops locally. Even rights of way can be altered over time. We are always grateful for information about any discrepancies between a guidebook and the facts on the ground, sent by email to info@cicerone.co.uk or by post to Cicerone, 2 Police Square, Milnthorpe LA7 7PY, United Kingdom.

*Front cover:* High on the cobbles of Gold Hill (Route 16)

# Contents

## INTRODUCTION                                                         13

▲ Grade 1        ▲ Grade 2        ▲ Grade 3        ▲ Grade 4        ▲ Grade 5

**GPX FILES**

GPX files for all routes can be downloaded for free at
**www.cicerone.co.uk/member**

## Symbols on the route maps

~ route

~ alternative route

> route direction

> alternative route direction

 start/finish point

‹12⟳› route link

➊→ stage number

�’ bike shop

☕ pub

☕ café

## Features on the overview map

 Urban area

National Park

Area of Outstanding Natural Beauty

800m
600m
400m
200m
75m
0m

The route maps in this guide are reproduced at 1:250,000
(1cm = 2.5km)

0        2.5        5 km
0    1    2    3   miles

## ROUTE GRADES AND ABBREVIATIONS

Routes in this guide are graded as follows:

▲ perfect for cadence work with just the odd climb along the way

▲▲ a little lumpier but plenty of recovery miles

▲▲▲ quality hill-time with some sharp and testy climbs

▲▲▲ no retreat – no surrender

▲▲▲ carry a white handkerchief in your back pocket

The following symbols are used in the route descriptions:

↑ straight ahead

← left

→ right

↰ left-hand

↱ right-hand

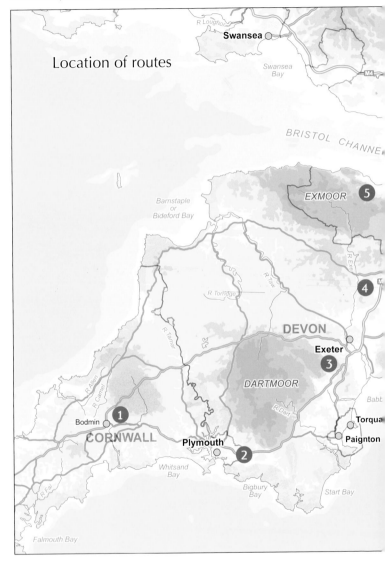

## ROUTE SUMMARY TABLE

| Route | Title | Location(s) | Start/Finish | Distance | Ascent | Grade | Time | Page |
|---|---|---|---|---|---|---|---|---|
| 1 | Atlantic Roller | Cornwall | Dragon Leisure Centre, Bodmin SX 077 653 | 119km (74 miles) | 2040m (6695ft) | ▲ | 5hrs–6hrs 30mins | 29 |
| 2 | Tor de Moor | Dartmoor | Ivybridge Leisure Centre long stay car park, Ivybridge SX 635 560 | 78km (48½ miles) | 1600m (5250ft) | ▲ | 3hrs–4hrs 30mins | 35 |
| 3 | King of the Castle | Dartmoor | Haldon Forest Park, Bullers Hill, Exeter SX 885 847 | 58.75km (36½ miles) | 1035m (3395ft) | ▲ | 2hrs 30mins– 3hrs 30mins | 38 |
| 4 | Exe-Factor | Exmoor | Exe Valley Leisure Centre, Tiverton SS 954 134 | 76km (47¼ miles) | 1630m (5350ft) | ▲ | 3hrs 30mins– 5hrs | 41 |
| 5 | Slam Dunk | Exmoor | Long stay car park, Dunster SS 994 439 | 89.75km (55¾ miles) | 2155m (7070ft) | ▲ | 4hrs 30mins– 6hrs | 45 |
| 6 | Blackdown Hills | Somerset and Devon | Blackbrook Pavilion car park, Taunton ST 247 239 | 76.5km (47½ miles) | 1235m (4050ft) | ▲ | 3hrs 30mins– 4hrs 30mins | 49 |
| 7 | A Ridge too Far | Somerset | Wellington Sports Centre, Wellington ST 131 208 | 105.5km (65½ miles) | 1600m (5250ft) | ▲ | 4hrs 30mins– 6hrs | 53 |
| 8 | Weston-super-Nightmare | Somerset | Hutton Moor Leisure Centre, Weston-super-Mare ST 340 611 | 89.75km (55¾ miles) | 880m (2885ft) | ▲ | 3hrs 30mins– 5hrs | 59 |
| 9 | Mid-Somer Murder | Somerset | Wells Leisure Centre, Wells ST 536 461 | 87.75km (54½ miles) | 850m (2790ft) | ▲ | 3hrs 30mins– 5hrs | 63 |
| 10 | Mendip Madness | Somerset | Hengrove Park Leisure Complex, Bristol ST 593 688 | 90km (56 miles) | 1270m (4165ft) | ▲ | 4hrs– 5hrs 30mins | 69 |

▲ Grade 1     ▲ Grade 2     ▲ Grade 3     ▲ Grade 4     ▲ Grade 5

| Route | Title | Location(s) | Start/Finish | Distance | Ascent | Grade | Time | Page |
|---|---|---|---|---|---|---|---|---|
| 11 | Over the Edge | Gloucs | Yate Leisure Centre, Yate ST 713 825 | 101.5km (63 miles) | 1335m (4380ft) | ▲ | 4hrs–5hrs 30mins | 73 |
| 12 | Forest of Dean | Gloucs | Chepstow Leisure Centre, Chepstow ST 526 945 | 93.25km (58 miles) | 1590m (5215ft) | ▲ | 4hrs–5hrs 30mins | 79 |
| 13 | Cotswold Caper | Cotswolds | Cotswold Leisure Centre, Cirencester SP 019 018 | 108km (67 miles) | 1425m (4675ft) | ▲ | 4hrs 30mins–6hrs | 82 |
| 14 | Fool Hardy | Dorset | Top O'Town car park, Dorchester ST 688 907 | 98.5km (61¼ miles) | 1235m (4050ft) | ▲ | 4hrs–5hrs 30mins | 88 |
| 15 | Jurassic Classic | Dorset | Sandbanks Ferry Terminal, Poole SZ 036 871 | 89.5km (55½ miles) | 870m (2855ft) | ▲ | 3hrs 30mins–5hrs | 93 |
| 16 | Thrill of the Chase | Dorset | Queen Elizabeth Leisure Centre, Wimborne Minster ST 998 006 | 89.75km (55¾ miles) | 785m (2575ft) | ▲ | 3hrs 30mins–5hrs | 98 |
| 17 | Zig Zag | Wiltshire and Dorset | Five Rivers Leisure Centre, Salisbury ST 138 302 | 104.5km (65½ miles) | 1235m (4050ft) | ▲ | 4hrs–5hrs 30mins | 103 |
| 18 | Plain Sailing | Wiltshire | Five Rivers Leisure Centre, Salisbury ST 138 302 | 70km (43½ miles) | 575m (1885ft) | ▲ | 2hrs 30mins–3hrs 30mins | 108 |
| 19 | Cheval Blanc | Wiltshire | Lime Kiln Leisure Centre, Royal Wootton Bassett SU 069 830 | 68km (42¼ miles) | 595m (1950ft) | ▲ | 2hrs 30mins–3hrs 30mins | 111 |
| 20 | Clyffe Hanger | Wiltshire | Lime Kiln Leisure Centre, Royal Wootton Bassett SU 069 830 | 104km (64¾ miles) | 635m (2085ft) | ▲ | 3hrs 30mins–5hrs | 115 |

Two is always better than one (on Route 17)

# Introduction

Sportive cycling is enjoying a boom time. From chip-timed monumental feats of organisation and logistics to small club-run affairs; cycle sportives create a buzz all of their own. The UK cycling calendar enjoys a series of year-round sportive events, as thousands of cyclists – from social riders to wannabe racers – participate every weekend in this most challenging of cycle sports. Whether it is to improve on a time achieved on an earlier attempt, or only to discover some of the UK's most exciting terrain, no other cycling activity can compare with the challenge, friendliness and organisation of today's sportive events.

With the recent and ongoing successes of many of the UK's cycling heroes and heroines in the Olympics, World Championships and the Tour de France, men and women have taken to road cycling in numbers not seen since the Victorian era. With the likes of Sir Chris Hoy, Sir Bradley Wiggins, Victoria Pendleton, Chris Froome and Laura Trott filling the back pages of daily newspapers, UK cyclists are now as recognisable today as any other major sporting stars.

Maybe not maintaining a shoulder to shoulder pace with such stellar names, we mere mortal riders who hit the road – dragging ourselves out of bed at unearthly hours every weekend, to ride in all weathers – take our pleasure from cycle sportives in many different ways: fitness training, life challenges, cycling obsession or raising money for charity. Whatever the reason, the routes in this guide offer riders of all abilities the perfect opportunity to train for their chosen sportive event, by pitching themselves against the most challenging and scenic areas that the south west of England has to offer.

Approaching Corfe Castle from Church Knowle (Route 15)

## About sportives

A sportive often includes a number of routes ranging from 25 miles up to 100 miles, or further. The varying route options enable riders of all abilities to challenge themselves against the clock without having to live by a strict training regime. Sportives are normally held on open roads and riders must obey the Highway Code. Each route will be well signposted by the organisers with strategically placed feed and drink stations peppered along the way. Most sportives now include chip-timing to accurately record the time of individual riders.

Arguably, the UK sportive scene has grown organically from a combination of the French 'randonnée cyclosportive' scene and British cycle club endurance rides. For many years cyclists have flocked, in their thousands, to participate in both open and closed road events over some of the toughest mountains in continental Europe. Some might say that modern British sportives are more akin to cycle club 'reliability trials'.

Popular during the winter months, reliability trials are long-distance club rides where riders and club racers concentrate on getting more 'relaxed or social' miles into their legs. Club runs seldom use route signage or feed stations, so riders are left to fend for themselves (hence, 'reliability'). Café stops are often an integral and important port of call during club runs.

Whatever the reasons, the ever-growing UK sportive season enjoys a calendar full of exciting and challenging rides in some of the most beautiful landscapes that these islands have to offer.

There is also a growing number of sportive events in the UK that are held on closed roads. Events such as the 'Etape Cymru' in North Wales and the 'Prudential London–Surrey 100' prove to be hugely popular, with riders entering in their thousands to

Your riding partner: the best accessory yet

complete these arduous rides in the safety of closed roads. But distance is not the only challenge facing sportive riders – hills play a major part in sportive rides, and conquering a severe climb is seen as one of the real tests of any given event. Sportives may not yet attract the mad-cap cycling supporters, or *tifosi*, as seen lining the mountain stages of the Tour de France, but a warm welcome is always on hand at the end of a sportive event.

Although sportive events are not races, many riders pride themselves in getting around in the quickest time possible and will look to improve on their times throughout the season. But one thing's for sure, sportive riders can enjoy a sense of achievement that few other amateur cyclists can. A hundred miles is a long way and should never be taken lightly. Train for the distance, train for the hills – enjoy the ride.

## The south west of England

Within the UK's political structure, the counties of Cornwall, Devon, Dorset, Somerset, Gloucestershire and Wiltshire combine to complete the jigsaw of the English south west peninsula. It is a region most famous for its myths and legends: from King Arthur's castle at Tintagel to Glastonbury's foreboding tor, England's south west is home to many of its most fabled tales. With its enviable warm climate and soft sandy beaches, the region is also the UK's most popular holiday destination. So if you've packed the car full with

buckets and spades and kids, don't forget your bike!

To top it all, the peninsula offers a series of stunning areas that might have been created purely for the delights of sportive cycling. With great destinations such as Dartmoor, Exmoor and the Forest of Dean on the menu, sportive cycle training in England's south west takes on a sense of adventure that few other regions can provide.

The most dominating feature of the region for sportive cyclists is the proximity of so many superb hills. There are just too many of them to list here, but be prepared to experience hill climbing and descending that will turn the most reticent of cyclists into mountain goats. Be cautious, however, as conditions on the hills are changeable and they can be deceptive to the unwary. Beginners should take on the lower-grade routes in this book first to get some easier miles into their legs, then tackle the higher-grade routes, which feature the guide's most major and challenging climbs. Ride to your heart's content – or until your legs give out!

## Getting there and getting around

*By car*

Gloucestershire, Somerset and Wiltshire are easily accessed from London via the main arterial route of the M4, and from England's north and Midlands via the M5. The M5 provides

Tarr Steps require dismount and careful crossing (Route 4)

further access to even the remotest parts of England's south west peninsula, and the A30 and A38 roads are well placed to venture into Cornwall.

Other major roads servicing the region include the M3 and the A303, which, together, form a route that leads from London towards Exeter, passing iconic Stonehenge along the way. Most areas of Dorset and East Devon are easily accessed via the M3 and M27 through Hampshire to the A31 and A35 roads.

*By rail*

Riders wishing to travel to the region by train should first check out National Rail enquiries (go to www.nationalrail.co.uk and click on 'Cyclists'). Here you will find easy links to your nearest regional train provider and information on how you can book

your bike onto a train. Gateway train destinations tend to be Bristol or Exeter, where a change of train might be required.

## When to go

The south west of England enjoys a mild climate most of the year round, and the further south and west you go, the milder it gets. It is quite normal to see semi-exotic plants and trees in Devon and Cornwall, especially along the more sheltered south coast. But the region is also home to some pretty unforgiving high moorland areas that should never be treated lightly – even in summer.

Dartmoor and Exmoor can be brutally exposed and, being high mountain regions, the weather here can change very quickly. Always carry suitable emergency clothing with you, like a lightweight waterproof top. On the high moors, visibility can be a problem too, so wear something bright and ride with caution; a small set of clip-on emergency lights will add almost no weight to your bike, but they could quite easily help avoid any nasty situations in bad weather.

## Accommodation

Being a large holiday destination, there is usually no shortage of options when selecting from available accommodation. Leave it too late in the summer or at holiday times, however, and booking can be a bit of a nightmare. Bed and breakfast accommodation is a firm favourite anywhere in England's south west and, with the advent of www.airbnb.co.uk, the selection of excellent short-notice overnight accommodation has been greatly enhanced. See Appendix B for a list of accommodation websites.

There's no shortage of interesting cities, towns and villages in which to base yourself while exploring the region. The historic port of Plymouth works equally well for Atlantic Roller and Tor de Moor, while Exeter is the perfect base for King of the Castle. The bustling market town of Tiverton is an obvious choice for Exe-Factor and Slam Dunk, if you combine the two routes together, and either Wellington or Taunton act as an ideal launch pad for Blackdown Hills and A Ridge too Far.

The ancient cathedral city of Wells is well situated for any of the three routes that cover the Mendip Hills – Weston-super-Nightmare, Mid-Somer Murder and Mendip Madness. In Gloucestershire, Cirencester, Cheltenham or Chepstow offer riders a wealth of local interest and accommodation from which to enhance the ride experiences of Over the Edge, Forest of Dean and Cotswold Caper. Both Dorchester and Poole are natural choices for the Dorset routes – Fool Hardy, Jurassic Classic and Thrill of the Chase – while Salisbury is a terrific city from which to explore the chalk valleys of Wiltshire on Zig Zag and Plain Sailing. Further north, Marlborough and Royal Wootton Bassett hold plenty of cultural interest as well as being springboards for Cheval Blanc and Clyffe Hanger.

Blue sky riding en route to Alvediston (Route 17)

A friendly spectator at Combe St Nicholas (Route 6)

## On the road

*Hills*

England's south west is teeming with hills – even the mostly flat routes in this guide have at least some hilly sections. But, love them or hate them, you'll just have to get used to them if you're going to ride cycle sportives. Riding 50, 80 or even 100 miles can be a real test, but adding a series of long, grinding ascents and lung-busting climbs into any ride will drag the difficulty factor kicking and screaming into a whole new realm.

Some routes in this book, such as Slam Dunk and Zig Zag, are all about hill climbing. Every now and again it's worth the effort to include harder climbing routes as a specific training ride. It's also worth remembering that a challenging climb at the start of an event with fresh legs will feel like a very different beast after 50 miles or so. There are no shortcuts to hill climbing;

seek them out, train on them regularly and beat them. To avoid the walk of shame during an event, train for the hills at every opportunity.

Yes, it would be naive to enter a ride such as the Fred Whitton Challenge in the Lake District and endure some of the most challenging climbs in England without suitable training. But there are plenty of challenging hills to be found in the south west of the country too, just don't get caught out by a lack of quality hill training. Plan ahead, choose your routes carefully and make sure you know what you are getting into.

Read through this book, train on the routes that suit your aspirations and fitness, and, as you progress through your training schedule, select tougher routes on which to train. Following the routes in this guidebook is also a great way to explore the varied and beautiful countryside of England's south west. Take your

## SAFETY

Cycle sportives and training rides are not races, and, unless it is held on closed roads, a sportive event and its competitors are bound by current traffic regulations and the Highway Code. Therefore it's worth getting into some good riding habits from the outset of your training regime. This will pay good dividends in your safety cycle-management come the day of the event.

Keep your bike in **good working order**, especially if you're getting in plenty of winter miles. Regular servicing of it is always a good thing, as is cleaning. Cleaning your bike is a good opportunity for close inspection, thereby avoiding potential problems later on. Check tyre pressures regularly too; correct tyre pressures are often the difference between an efficient and enjoyable ride and a puncture-fraught journey.

**Be seen** by other road users. Wear at least one item of bright clothing and always fit a rear light. It's often as difficult to be seen on a bright sunny day as it is on a cloudy, overcast day. Always wear a cycle helmet.

**Ride courteously**, keep other road users in mind and give clear indications and signals of your intentions. Always check over your shoulder before you manoeuvre.

**Be self sufficient** as much as possible. As a minimum of self-help and self-reliance, learn how to make small adjustments to your bike, repair punctures and fix a broken chain in the comfort of your home – don't leave it till it happens out on the road. See Appendix A for a list of bike shops.

### Suggested minimum repair kit:

- pump
- $CO_2$ cartridges (x2) and inflator
- tyre levers (x3)
- spare tubes (x2)
- tube repair patches or puncture repair kit
- tyre repair patches
- multi-tool
- chain tool

### Other essential items and considerations:

- fully charged mobile phone
- paper cash
- debit or credit card (taxi ride back to the start?)
- a riding partner or two
- let someone know where you are going and how long you're likely to be away

## EMERGENCIES

Should a **serious injury** occur while out on a ride and you require hospital treatment, **dial 999 and request an ambulance**. Give them your location and the state of your injuries. Always carry a fully charged mobile phone with you when riding.

If your injuries are less serious then consider calling 111 for the NHS urgent care facility. If you feel you are able to make it to an Accident and Emergency (A&E) unit, see Appendix B for a list of local hospitals with full A&E facilities.

time, enjoy your riding and build up your distances and challenges before letting yourself loose on the world of cycle sportives.

### Singletrack lanes
These are great for deterring lorries, but the myriad narrow lanes that cover the region will often be loose and gravelly under your wheels. They will also be slippery with mud in the rain and, inevitably, the only vehicle you'll meet will be a delivery van in a hurry. Treat singletrack lanes with respect: keep your speed down on descents, ride in single file, give the rider in front some space and expect the unexpected.

### Cattle grids
These beauties pop-up frequently, especially in and around the national parks. They pose no problem as such, but it's always worth crossing them with a degree of caution when wet. Always cross them straight-on. Keeping a little momentum to free-wheel over cattle grids helps, especially when approaching from uphill, and standing up as you rattle across reduces weight on the back wheel to lessen pinch-flats and is kinder on your spine!

## Equipment

### The bike
It may not be 'all about the bike', but a good-quality, lightweight road bike certainly makes life easier out on the road. A lightweight bike will pay dividends when pedalling uphill and will be easier, generally, to propel along the road than a heavier one.

Make sure you ride a bike that is the right size for you; this is important if you want to get the maximum power output from your bike and avoid any injuries. If too small, it will be cramped, uncomfortable and will not allow efficient pedalling; if too big, it will stretch you out and you may well end up with back problems. A bike that is too large may also not allow enough stand-over height, which is potentially dangerous, and the handlebars will be too far away to easily reach for the brake levers. Take the time to get along to your local bike shop for specialist advice and to get sized up properly.

### Helmet

Always wear a properly fitted cycle helmet. There are plenty of light-weight, good-quality helmets out there in the market to satisfy even the most reticent of helmet sceptics. You will wear it a great deal and, more than likely, you will have to wear one to ride in an organised sportive anyway. Buy a good-quality helmet (do not scrimp), ensuring that it fits correctly and is comfortable from the very out-set, and look after it. You only have one head, so use it wisely. Again, get some advice and proper fitting from your local bike shop.

### Cycle shorts

Always buy the best cycle shorts that you can afford: 100 miles is a long way to be sat on a saddle and your rear will thank you for investing wisely. Bib shorts are worth considering; they are extremely comfortable and don't cut into your waist at all. If you are riding often, ideally you should invest in two or three pairs. Wash them regularly, and don't wear underwear under-neath them.

### Pedals and shoes

Clipless pedals and shoes are proven to be far more efficient than traditional pedals without straps. If you do get into sportive cycling quite seriously and begin to include high mileage routes into your training programme, then specialist clipless shoes – such as Shimano Road SPDs – are worth their weight in gold.

### Cycling apparel

There's a whole world of fashionable and attractive cycling tops out there on the market waiting to catch your eye. Some of the prices will make your eyes water too, but there's no need to go crazy with the latest trend, as a steady supply of hard-wearing and close-fitting cycle tops are readily available at less than bank-breaking prices. Invest wisely in your cycling tops; buy the best that you can afford and only buy specific cycling jerseys made from either man-made fabrics, such as Polyester, or, in some cases, natural materials like Merino Wool,

Be seen – be safe!

if retro styling is your bag. It's worth having a selection of short- and long-sleeve jerseys, to allow for warm or cold weather. Make sure all tops you buy have at least a neck zip and a couple of rear pockets.

When the weather turns cool it's worth considering layering up both upper body and legs. Long-sleeve tops and cycling leggings will keep hard-working muscles warm, and a windproof and waterproof cycling jacket is a must. Less bulky items allow you to roll them up and place them in a rear pocket while you're warm. Buy kit that will put up with the rigours of constant washing and drying.

Cycling gloves are are a must-have item too; not only will they keep your hands warm but they soak up the sweat from your palms and help keep a safe grip on the handlebars. Wear short-fingered gloves when warm and full-fingered ones when cool. Waterproof cycling gloves should be considered in the winter or heavy rain conditions.

Cycle-specific glasses are highly recommended too: a fly in the eye at 20mph is not funny. Get clear lenses for rainy days, yellow lenses for low-light days and sunglasses for days when the sun decides to show its face. Three-in-one options are readily available so, unless you want to, it isn't necessary to buy three separate pairs.

## Bike maintenance

Clean your bike regularly, preferably after each ride, but do so especially if the weather was inclement on your last ride. Grit and crud from the road will wear out your chain and components in no time if you don't wash them off. Wash the bike with warm soapy water after each ride, dry it off and lightly lube the chain. This simple routine will work wonders at prolonging the life of your bike, and will save you money in the long run.

When you get down into areas such as the spokes or bottom bracket, it's easier to inspect them as you clean your bike. Check the frame for cracks or anything that looks out of the ordinary. Check bolts regularly for tightness too; don't over-tighten them but always check for safety.

Treat your bike to a service at least twice a year by a specialist bike shop (until you have the cables changed you won't realise just how hard your gear selection has become). Put a new chain on too; it won't last as long as the cassette but by replacing the chain you will prolong the life of the complete drive chain. When to service your bike may depend on how many miles you're putting in, but after a long winter or in the run-up to the sportive season, it's worth giving it some TLC so that it's ready for your event.

## The rules of the road

Cyclists are responsible for their own behaviour on the road and are therefore bound by the Highway Code. Ride responsibly and be courteous to other road users, especially

Keep your eyes peeled for National
Cycle Network route signage

More than one route features a stretch
boasting a descent ratio of one in three

Safety first – always!

pedestrians and horse riders (always
give way). Always give clear indications as to your intentions before
manoeuvring; the driver behind you
is not a mind reader, so indicate in
plenty of time before turning.

Look over your right shoulder to
check behind you before manoeuvring, turning and moving out into
traffic; this small but very important
act is your greatest asset in road safety
and could prevent anything nasty
from happening. Don't drift in and
out of stationary traffic; stay out in
the road so people in other vehicles
can see you. Try not to ride too close
to the kerb side of the road either;
there are drains and potholes waiting
to eat you up. You will also be seen
much earlier on a bend if you stay
out from the edge. How you behave
will reflect how other road users view
other cyclists. Be an ambassador for
your sport by riding responsibly – and
remember to smile and wave (or at
least nod) to other cyclists... please!

## Navigation

The navigation in this guidebook
is designed to be as intuitive and
straightforward as possible. While
none are onerous, some routes are
easier to navigate than others. While
clearly not in the game of stopping
unnecessarily, there may be times
when a quick reference to the route
guide is required. If you've downloaded the route into your GPS,
smartphone or other navigation aid,
so much the better. Keep the book

## MAPS

All the required OS Landranger maps (1:50,000) for this guide can be found as follows:

- 162 Gloucester & Forest of Dean
- 163 Cheltenham & Cirencester
- 172 Bristol & Bath
- 173 Swindon & Devizes
- 181 Minehead & Brendon Hills
- 182 Weston-super-Mare
- 183 Yeovil & Frome
- 184 Salisbury & The Plain
- 191 Okehampton & North Dartmoor
- 192 Exeter & Sidmouth
- 193 Taunton & Lyme Regis
- 194 Dorchester & Weymouth
- 195 Bournemouth & Purbeck
- 200 Newquay & Bodmin
- 201 Plymouth & Launceston
- 202 Torbay & South Dartmoor

Welcome to Devon, and Hemyock

handy when out on a ride but remember: never read a map or guidebook while moving; always pull over first.

In lieu of direction arrows that would guide you around a sportive event, normal road signage now becomes your replacement arrows. The road signage throughout the routes in this guide is generally well maintained, but there's always the chance that now and again one will try to trip you up with washed-out lettering. It's important to spend time studying the routes beforehand to help familiarise yourself with the ride.

Bear in mind that chatting away to your ride partner can cause wrong turns to be taken. Speed is another reason to miss a turn – going too fast downhill or pedalling hard with your head down results in a loss of concentration and missing that all-important junction. Remember: these rides are training routes, not races. Stay in control of your bike, look where you're going, enjoy the beautiful scenery – and check the signage.

## Feed stations

As the only power source for your bike, you need to refuel yourself during a ride. Pubs, village shops, post offices, garages and cafés act as food and drink stations. Regardless of distance, any ride can feel like a long way from home when it's cold, wet and windy, especially on the high moors of Exmoor and Dartmoor. Don't make it any harder for yourself by cycling on an empty tank.

Carry plenty of food, water and energy bars (bars and gels can be crammed into rear pockets or stuffed into small feedbags on your bike). Top-up water bottles at every opportunity and refuel as you ride. Also remember that it's important to be self-reliant as much as possible; some pubs or cafés en route may not be open if you're heading out in the early morning.

The old training maxim applies to everyone: drink before you're thirsty and eat before you're hungry. Keep your energy levels up and replenish little and often as you go along – your performance and recovery levels will benefit dramatically.

## Using this guide

Cycle sportive events often cater for two or three distances: 100 miles, 50 miles or even fewer, and, depending on the rider's aspirations and fitness levels, a suitable route can be chosen. The routes in this guidebook are designed to offer a happy medium across the distances involved and, importantly, provide some insight into what to expect when covering longer and more challenging distances by road bike.

Each route is designed for both newcomers and experienced sportive riders alike. Having built up a base level of fitness and stamina, any fledgling sportive riders will soon feel the benefit of testing themselves against the distances and terrain involved. More experienced riders will enjoy the challenging nature of this region and the opportunity to discover new routes on which to test themselves

Build it into your training regime: Tea, jam and clotted cream

Time for a tea break at Guiting Power (Route 13)

in the most scenic areas of England's south west.

As in any well organised sportive route, the majority of mileage covered in this guide is on quiet country roads and lanes. B roads are kept to a minimum and are generally quiet as far as traffic is concerned. Major road sections are only used when unavoidable but integral to the route. Right-hand turns, especially on A and B roads, are kept to a minimum and used only where necessary. As nice as it might seem, it would be near impossible to have left-hand turns only and still create a worthwhile route.

Just like anywhere else in the UK, the quality of road surfaces in England's south west is a lottery. From mud-covered farm tracks to fresh licks of tarmac, you will encounter every type of surface. It's also worth noting that the class of road often has no reflection on its state of repair.

All the routes in this guide can be downloaded and are compatible for GPS. Each route is original in its concept, is the creation of the author, and is designed to cover areas in which sportive rides are popular. Any similarity to existing sportive events is purely coincidental. The intention is also that the routes should be as close as possible to built-up areas. Not every route needs to be a 'destination' ride but, if you're lucky enough to live close to a route, riders can start from a more convenient point.

Route maps and profiles show you what to expect during each ride, and refreshment stops and bike shops have been plotted onto the maps with easy-to-spot icons. The route summary table at the start of the guide gives an overview detailing the basics of the 20 routes: location, start and finish point, distance, ascent, grade and approximate time. Appendix A lists bike shops and cycle repair outfits on a route-by-route basis, should you have any bike maintenance emergencies. Appendix B lists useful websites for sportive organisations and accommodation, as well as contact details for local hospitals.

## Timings

Timing are subjective and should only be used as a guide: café stops, puncture repairs, fitness levels, type of terrain (hilly rather than flat) and weather conditions are just a few internal and external influences on the time taken to ride a particular route.

There will always be exceptions to the rule, of course. if Chris Froome finds himself holidaying in Cornwall, he could rightly expect to set a premium time for Atlantic Roller.

## Cadence

Performance cycling is all about optimising efficiency, and cadence is the cycling term for RPM (revolutions per minute). If cyclists turns their pedals at one rotation per second, they are deemed to be working at 60 RPM. Other factors do come into play, however: the selected gear, whether the terrain is rough or smooth and whether going up or down a hill, or even the weather conditions – especially the wind.

All these factors play their part in how cyclists ride. Ultimately, the desire is to pedal as smoothly and

The Blackdown Hills: once ridden, never forgotten (Route 6)

The roads less travelled: the Isle of Purbeck in all its glory (Route 15)

efficiently as possible to get the greatest return for the effort put in. It is better to spin the pedals efficiently rather than churn out a big gear and simply burn out the legs in no time.

Keep a higher cadence for more efficient pedalling, and aim for somewhere between 80 to 100 RPM. Don't worry too much about the speed at first, work on cycling efficiently; over a long distance a high cadence is the most effective way to ride.

## Linking up routes

For riders who really want to test themselves before an event, many routes in this guidebook are purposely located so that they can be easily joined together, should the legs be willing. This is especially useful for riders who are training for a 100-mile event (or even longer), who need to test their legs, lungs and mental attitude towards such endurance events. The route links have their own icons on the maps.

# Route 1
*Atlantic Roller (Cornwall)*

| | |
|---|---|
| **Start/Finish** | Dragon Leisure Centre, Bodmin SX 077 653 |
| **Distance** | 119km (74 miles) |
| **Ascent** | 2040m (6695ft) |
| **Grade** | |
| **Time** | 5hrs–6hrs 30mins |
| **Feed stations** | The Sandbar Café, Polzeath; Camelot Castle Hotel, Tintagel; The Rising Sun Inn, Altarnun; The CheeseWring Hotel, Minions |
| **Access** | From the large roundabout on the junction of the A38/A30 at Bodmin, take the exit onto Carminow Road, signposted Industrial Estates. Go over the narrow railway bridge, continue to a T-junction and turn L onto the B3268. At a mini roundabout, turn R into the leisure centre. |

Atlantic Roller is a feast of mythical landscapes and dramatic coastal scenery, and it harbours enough climbing to satisfy the most ardent of sportive riders. The ascents are demanding, but the rewards? Breathtaking. With Arthurian legend and plenty of ancient Celtic crosses to mark the way, Cornwall's history and culture comes thick and fast, just like the mist on Bodmin Moor.

## Overview

After an initial steep climb out of Bodmin, the journey north covers undulating countryside before the route then delves deep into the Atlantic coastline at Polzeath. Further steady going along the north Cornish coast leads to the ruins of Tintagel – a sensational setting for a tea stop. Close-knit contours and eerie landscapes fill the senses thereafter, as the hills become less forgiving and line themselves up to drain your energy. Beyond Minions and a final hilly flourish, the welcoming long, rolling descent into Bodmin is your reward for all that hard work.

**1** Exit ← from the leisure centre in **Bodmin** and follow Lostwithiel Road to the roundabout at the bottom of the hill in the town centre. Turn ← at the roundabout and take the first → up Castle Street. Continue to the road junction just before the **A30** and turn ←, signposted Helland. Continue along the narrow road to a road junction at **Merry Meeting** and turn ← for Wadebridge and St Mabyn. Go over the River Camel

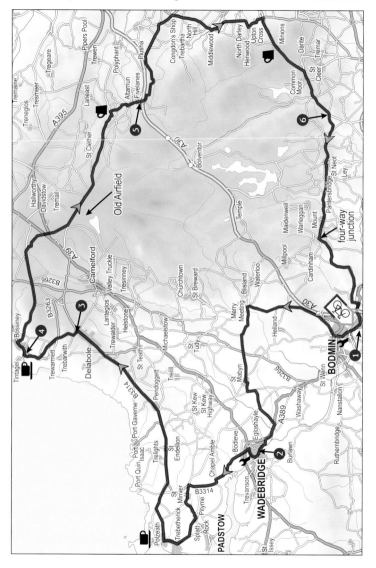

Polzeath: life's a beach and then you ride

then cross the **B3266** into **St Mabyn**. Turn ← opposite the cross onto Wadebridge Road, continue to the **A389** and turn →. On entering **Wadebridge**, turn ← towards the church tower.

**2** Follow the road to the mini roundabout beside the old bridge on the River Camel; turn → and climb to the next roundabout. Turn ← onto the **B3314**, signposted Rock and St Minver. Follow the B3314 over the **A39** to a crossroads adjacent to St Minver and turn ←. Continue through **St Minver** to the Pityme Inn and turn → onto Rock Road. Follow this road through **Trebetherick** and descend into **Polzeath**. After climbing out of Polzeath, continue to a double ← junction and take the second turning, signposted St Endellion, Port Isaac and Delabole. Continue to the junction with the B3314 and turn ← for the next 10km.

**3** On exiting **Delabole**, and in full view of the wind farm, turn ←, signposted Trebarwith. Turn → at the next junction (marked by a blue sign reading 'Unsuitable for long vehicles') and descend to a T-junction with the **B3263**. Turn ← and continue to the roundabout in **Tintagel**. Turn ← to reach Camelot Castle Hotel, overlooking Tintagel Head. Return to the roundabout, turn ← and follow the B3263 for 1km to **Bossiney**.

**4** Turn → in Bossiney, signposted Trevillet and Launceston, continue to the crossroads with the **B3266** and go ↑. Continue to the road junction beneath the giant pylons and turn ➡, signposted Camelford (A39). Cross ⬆ over both the **A39** and the **A395** to go past a factory-like dairy to reach a T-junction on the **old airfield**. Turn ⬅ and follow the road to the Rising Sun Inn. Go past the pub and turn ➡ at the next junction into **Altarnun**.

**5** Turn ⬅ at the T-junction in **Fivelanes**, then ➡, then ⬅ again to go under the **A30**, signposted Tregirls, Trenilk and Trevague. At the mini roundabout turn ⬅ and follow the narrow lane to the B3257 at **Plusha**. Turn ➡ and follow the B3257 to the crossroads at **Congdon's Shop** and turn ➡ onto the B3254. Follow the B3254 over the River Lynher at **Middlewood**, climb up through **North Darley** to the crossroads at **Upton Cross** and turn ➡, signposted Minions. Go past the CheeseWring Hotel in **Minions** and follow the road past the signs for Golitha Falls to the next junction, signposted Trengale (Unsuitable for HGVs).

**6** Turn ➡ and descend the very narrow lane (ride with caution) to the T-junction at the bottom and turn ➡ over the River Fowey. Climb out of the valley, continue to the T-junction in **St Neot** and turn ➡. Go through St Neot and climb Tripp Hill to **Pantersbridge** and **Mount**; at the **four-way junction** beyond Mount, turn ⬅ for Bodmin. Follow this superb descent to the roundabout on the A38 and turn ➡ to go

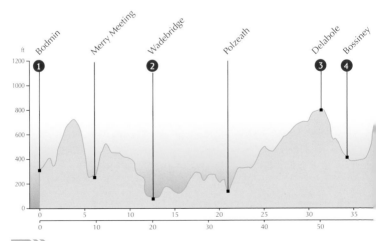

It's all downhill from here

over the **A30**. At the next roundabout turn ← onto Carminow Road, signposted Industrial Estates. Follow the road over the railway line to a T-junction with Lostwithiel Road and turn ← to return to the leisure centre in **Bodmin**.

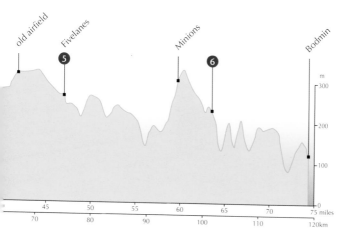

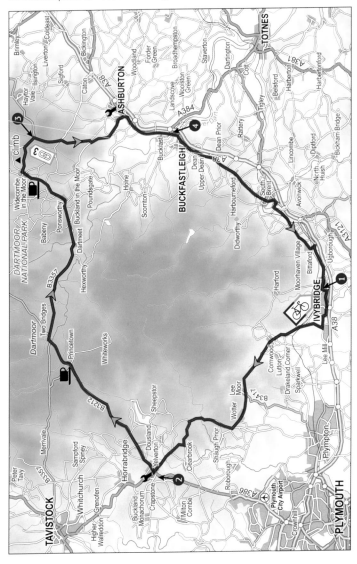

# Route 2
*Tor de Moor (Dartmoor)*

| | |
|---|---|
| **Start/Finish** | Ivybridge Leisure Centre long stay car park, Ivybridge SX 635 560 |
| **Distance** | 78km (48½ miles) |
| **Ascent** | 1600m (5250ft) |
| **Grade** | ▲▲▲ |
| **Time** | 3hrs–4hrs 30mins |
| **Feed stations** | Fox Tor Café, Princetown; Wayside Café, Widecombe in the Moor |
| **Access** | Take the Ivybridge exit off the A38 and follow the slip road to a roundabout. Exit onto Western Road and continue to the next roundabout. Turn R onto Marjorie Kelly Way and, at the next roundabout, take the first exit into the leisure centre car park. |

Part training ride, part adventure and altogether superb, Tor de Moor is as dramatic as it is challenging. Set in Dartmoor, one of the UK's classic cycling destinations, this route lets riders tick off the Tors one by one by riding along remote moorland roads between Dartmoor's granite giants.

## Overview

Without breaking sweat, the gentle ascent out of Ivybridge up onto Dartmoor National Park is an easy introduction to the drama that awaits you. The climb up from Yelverton into eerie Princetown, however, is almost as infamous to cyclists for its strenuousness as Princetown's Dartmoor Prison is to the public generally (and there is no escape from either!). A welcome break from climbing is soon provided, with a change of scenery in and around the tourist trap village of Widecombe in the Moor, before another classic climb up the B3387 reminds you of the route's overall difficulty grade. The long descent into Ashburton is just the tonic to recover, as is the final leg along the soft underbelly of Dartmoor back to Ivybridge.

**1** Exit ← from the car park in **Ivybridge**, turn → at the roundabout onto Marjorie Kelly Way and continue to the next roundabout. Turn ← onto Western Road, continue to another roundabout and go ↑ onto Cornwood Road (third exit). Where the cyclepath ends on Cornwood Road, turn ← onto Woodland Road and continue through **Cornwood**,

**Lee Moor** and **Wotter**. At the crossroads beyond Wotter, turn ➡, signposted Meavy and Yelverton. Follow the moorland road to the **A386** in **Yelverton**.

**2** Turn ➡ and go ⬆ at the roundabout onto the **B3212**, signposted Princetown. Follow the B3212 into **Princetown**, go ⬆ at the mini roundabout past Fox Tor Café to the T-junction with the **B3357**, and turn ➡. Cross the West Dart River at **Two Bridges** and follow the road as it becomes a steep descent into Dartmeet. Climb sharply out of **Dartmeet** to the road junction at the summit and turn ⬅, signposted Sherril and Babeny. Follow the road down into the valley to **Ponsworthy**, turn ⬅ over the ford and continue up the narrow lane to **Widecombe in the Moor**. Keep ⬅ at the church in Widecombe, follow the road around the back of the church – past the Wayside Café – and climb the B3387.

## Link to Route 3
After leaving **Widecombe in the Moor** and cresting the summit of the B3387, turn sharp ⬅ at the first road junction to join King of the Castle for true King of the Mountains training.

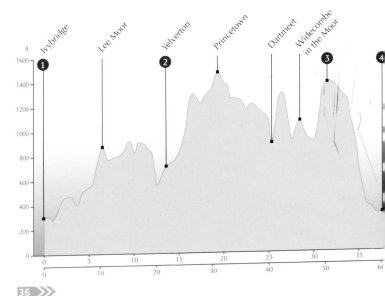

**3** After levelling out at the top of the climb, turn ➡, signposted Ashburton, and continue to a crossroads. Go ⬆ to continue descending to a T-junction. Turn ⬅ and descend into **Ashburton**. At the T-junction in the town centre, turn ➡ onto the B3352 and continue to another T-junction. Turn ⬅ and then, behind the petrol station, turn ➡ towards Buckfastleigh. At the T-junction with the B3380 in **Buckfastleigh**, turn ➡ to cross the River Dart, then turn ⬅ at the mini roundabout and follow the road through town.

**4** Continue following the road (it narrows through **Upper Dean**) to the T-junction in the centre of **South Brent**. Turn ⬅ to continue through town and carry on to another T-junction. Turn ➡ onto the B3372 then take the next ➡, signposted Brent Mill (along with a brown tourism sign and a sign for National Cycle Route 2). Follow the lane under the railway line to pick up the cycle route to Wrangaton and Bittaford. Go back under the railway line at **Bittaford** and turn ➡ onto the B3213. Continue to the roundabout in **Ivybridge** and turn ⬅. Continue to the next roundabout and take the third exit to return to the leisure centre car park.

# Route 3
## *King of the Castle (Dartmoor)*

| | |
|---|---|
| **Start/Finish** | Haldon Forest Park, Bullers Hill, Exeter SX 885 847 |
| **Distance** | 58.75km (36½ miles) |
| **Ascent** | 1035m (3395ft) |
| **Grade** |  |
| **Time** | 2hrs 30mins–3hrs 30mins |
| **Feed stations** | The Ridge Café, Haldon Forest Park; Hound of the Basket Meals, Hound Tor car park (seasonal); The Gateway Tea Room, Moretonhampstead |
| **Access** | Exit the A38 at Exeter Racecourse atop Haldon Hill and follow the brown tourist signs for Haldon Forest Park and Go Ape. |

Short, steep and very sweet, King of the Castle covers the best routes across eastern Dartmoor and works perfectly for those looking to up their mileage by linking to Tor de Moor.

## Overview

A near perfect freewheel into Chudleigh gets riders off to a great start before the dramatic scenery of Haytor comes into view. After Bovey Tracey the climb up to Haytor is as dramatic as it is tough, but the smooth, open moorland road cuts across the landscape like a slick race track before closing in again towards Hound Tor. The Hound of the Basket Meals mobile café at Hound Tor offers unlikely respite (weather permitting), while the sweeping road descent through Bridford Woods beyond Moretonhampstead into the Teign Valley is simply sublime – a true moment to savour. A gentle ride along the River Teign precedes the final climb up to the gleaming white beacon of Haldon Belvedere (Lawrence Castle) and the finish line.

**1** Exit the forest park and turn ➡ for 500m. At the crossroads turn ➡ to descend to the T-junction with the **B3344** in **Chudleigh**, and turn ➡. Cross over the **A38**, continue to the road junction and turn ➡ to follow the B3344 into **Chudleigh Knighton**. Turn ➡ again in Chudleigh Knighton onto The Chapelry, following the B3344 into **Bovey Tracey**. At the crossroads in Bovey Tracey, turn ⬅ over the River Bovey then, immediately after the Brookside Café, turn ⬅ again onto Newton Road.

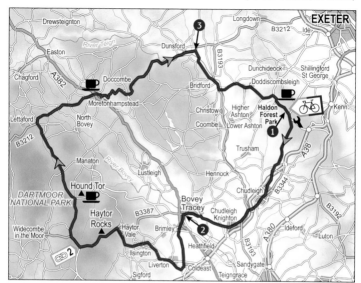

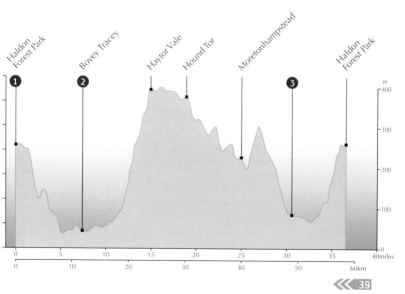

Turning right towards Hound Tor

**2** Follow Newton Road to the junction with Ashburton Road and turn
➡, then go over the **A382** to a crossroads and go ⬆. Continue to the
next crossroads, turn ➡ onto Old Liverton Road and climb gently to
**Ilsington**. Follow the road through the village and climb steadily to the
T-junction with the **B3387** in **Haytor Vale**. Turn ⬅ to climb past **Haytor
Rocks** and reach a road junction.

## Link to Route 2
Turn ⬅ here, signposted Ashburton, to join Tor de Moor for a full picture of
Dartmoor's delights.

Continue past the Ashburton turning to the next junction, and turn ➡ for
Hound Tor. Follow this road past **Hound Tor** car park to a T-junction with the
**B3212**, and turn ➡ for Moretonhampstead. At the crossroads with the **A382** in
**Moretonhampstead**, go ⬆ to continue through **Doccombe**. Around 2km after
crossing the River Teign, turn sharp ➡, signposted Christow and Chudleigh.

**3** Follow the River Teign to where the road becomes the **B3193**, and continue to a bridge. Turn ⬅ over the river into **Doddiscombsleigh**. Climb
up through the village to a T-junction and turn ⬅ towards Haldon
Belvedere (Lawrence Castle). At the T-junction below the castle turn ➡
and follow the road to reach Haldon Forest Park.

# Route 4
*Exe-Factor (Exmoor)*

| | |
|---|---|
| **Start/Finish** | Exe Valley Leisure Centre, Tiverton SS 954 134 |
| **Distance** | 76km (47¼ miles) |
| **Ascent** | 1630m (5350ft) |
| **Grade** | |
| **Time** | 3hrs 30mins–5hrs |
| **Feed stations** | Tarr Farm Inn, Tarr Steps; Bridge Cottage Tea Room, Winsford; The Tantivy Café, Dulverton |
| **Access** | Exit the M5 at Junction 27 and follow the A361 to the large roundabout at Tiverton. Turn L and go SA at the next roundabout onto Bolham Road. At the next roundabout turn L into the leisure centre car park. |

Everything that makes Mid Devon and Exmoor such exciting destinations for sportive cycling is encapsulated here in this compact training ride. The opening gambit from Tiverton is a gentle precursor before Exmoor quickly stamps its authority. With a dramatic river crossing and a couple of testing climbs, the southern areas of Exmoor National Park soon become an exciting playground that will test both fitness and determination. Thankfully, there are some great cafés en route in which to refuel, but enjoy the descents too; they're some of the finest to be found in the south west of England.

## Overview

The opening climb is so long and gentle you hardly notice the height gain, but once you've crossed the line into the national park the contours come thick and fast and offer little recovery time. The River Barle at Tarr Steps and the climb that follows are memorable moments for first-time visitors. A terrific descent into Winsford followed by a welcome pot of tea puts any pain onto the back-burner though. Steep climbing digs deep again at Exton, but long descents make all the uphills worth it. After a stiff climb out of Dulverton the gentle slopes of Bampton hold no horrors, and the final few miles back into Tiverton provide an excellent warm-down exercise.

**1** Exit the leisure centre car park in **Tiverton** and go ↑ at the roundabout onto Kennedy Way. Go past the hospital to the next roundabout, turn → onto Rackenford Road and follow it all the way to **Rackenford**.

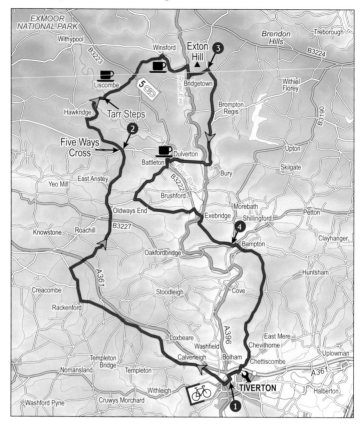

Just beyond the village, turn ➜, signposted Knowstone and Molland.
Continue to the next junction and turn ➜, signposted East Anstey.
Cross the **A361**, continue to the crossroads with the **B3227** and go ⬆
into **Oldways End**. Follow the road through the hamlet, continuing
towards East Anstey. At the road junction just before **East Anstey**, turn
➜, signposted Hawkridge and Tarr Steps, and climb to the T-junction at
**Five Ways Cross**.

With this sign at Five Ways Cross, you have been warned!

**2** Turn ← at the T-junction and then turn →, signposted Hawkridge and Tarr Steps. At the summit of the second climb (Colland Cross), turn → for **Hawkridge** and follow the road through the village towards Tarr Steps. Dismount at **Tarr Steps** and walk your bike carefully across the slabs, then climb to the crossroads with the **B3223**.

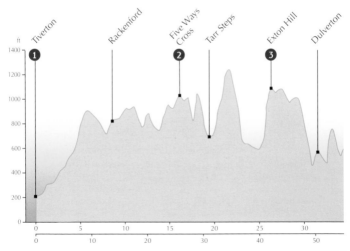

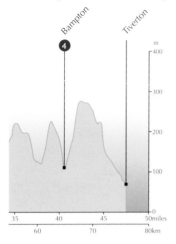

## Link to Route 5

For a truly monumental ride, turn ← onto the **B3223** and, at the next cross-roads, turn ← for **Withypool**, joining Slam Dunk.

Go ↑ at the crossroads and descend into **Winsford**. Just past the Bridge Cottage Tea Room, turn → and continue to the **A396**. Turn → into **Bridgetown** then turn sharp ← opposite the caravan park to climb steeply up through Exton and reach the T-junction at the summit of **Exton Hill**.

**3** Turn → and continue to a T-junction with the **A396**. Turn → and then ← onto the B3222 for Dulverton. Cross over the River Barle in **Dulverton**, turn → at **Battleton**, and continue to a T-junction. Turn ←, signposted Brushford and Bampton. Follow the long descent to the T-junction with the **B3222** and turn →, then cross the River Exe and turn → onto the **A396**. At the sharp ↱ bend, turn ← for Bampton. At the T-junction with the **B3227** in **Bampton**, turn ← and continue into the village centre.

**4** Follow the short one-way street (Back Street) to a T-junction. Turn → then immediately ← in front of the White Horse Inn (there really is a white horse above you) onto Brook Street and continue over the River Batherm. As you start to climb, turn ← (in effect ↑) up past the Quarryman's Rest pub onto National Cycle Network (NCN) Route 3. Follow the road to the T-junction beside the **A361** and turn ←. Cross the A361 and, at the next T-junction, turn →. Continue to the roundabout and turn ←. At the next roundabout, in **Tiverton**, turn ← into the leisure centre car park.

# Route 5
*Slam Dunk (Exmoor)*

| | |
|---|---|
| **Start/Finish** | Long stay car park, Dunster SS 994 439 |
| **Distance** | 89.75km (55¾ miles) |
| **Ascent** | 2155m (7070ft) |
| **Grade** | |
| **Time** | 4hrs 30mins–6hrs |
| **Feed stations** | Bridge Cottage Tea Room, Winsford; The Tea Rooms (old garage), Withypool; Home Cook Café, Porlock |
| **Access** | Exit the M5 at Junction 25 for Taunton and follow signs for the A358 (A39) towards Minehead. Leave the A39 at Dunster and turn L onto the A396. As you enter Dunster, turn L into the main car park. |

Slam Dunk is quite possibly the ultimate sportive – as long as hills are your thing. The toll road into Porlock offers the opportunity to experience some 'Alpine-esque' descending, before the route encounters a series of climbs that will stand you in good stead should you decide to hit the real Alps this season. There are some rewards to all that climbing too: long sweeping descents that leave you wanting more, dramatic views that take your breath away (weather permitting) and a smattering of cafés that provide a welcome haven in which to refuel tired legs and talk excitedly about the route already covered.

## Overview
After the long, steady climb from Timberscombe the open moorland sections between Exton and Porlock come at you like a runaway roller coaster. But this is only the beginning. The gritty challenges of Crawter Hill and Luccombe Hill, high on the broad shoulders of Dunkery Hill, put you through a true test of stamina and determination. The fast, sweeping descent from Wheddon Cross back to Dunster is a fitting final reward that is guaranteed to turn grimaces into grins.

**1** Exit the car park, turn ← and follow the A396 through **Dunster**. Continue to the junction for **Timberscombe** and turn ← onto Brook Street. At the Lion Inn, turn ← onto Church Street and climb to the crossroads with the **B3224**. Go ↑ and continue to a second road junction.

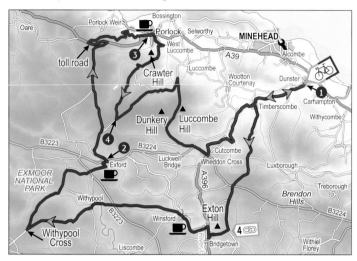

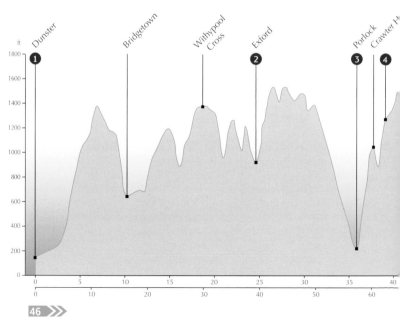

**Crossing the ford at Winsford**

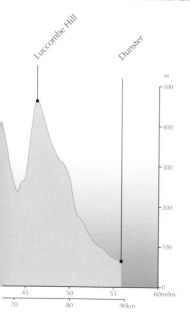

## Link to Route 4

Riders looking to gain a King of the Mountains shirt should go ↑ at this junction and join Exe-Factor.

Turn → to descend into Exton. At the T-junction with the **A396**, turn sharp →, and then turn ← for Winsford. Turn ← in **Winsford** to cross the ford (slippery when wet!) and then climb to the crossroads with the **B3223**. Go ↑ and descend into **Withypool**. Cross the River Barle and turn →, sign-posted Sandyway and South Molton. At the summit of the long climb, turn → at **Withypool Cross**, signposted Landacre. Descend to the River Barle and climb up to the crossroads with the **B3223**. Go ↑ and descend to the T-junction with the **B3224** in **Exford**.

Dunkery Hill – the best/worst is yet to come!

**2** Turn ➜ over the river, continue past the White Horse Inn, and turn ⬅ by the park onto Park Street. Continue past the park and climb sharply out of Exford. Follow the high moorland road towards Porlock until you reach the T-junction with the **A39**. Turn ⬅, climb to the next road junction and turn ➜, signposted Toll Road avoiding Porlock Hill (this is a much better way down – although it costs £1). Descend the toll road to the T-junction with the A39 at the foot of Porlock Hill and turn ⬅. Continue through **Porlock** to the car park opposite the red phone box.

**3** Turn ➜ immediately after the car park, signposted Doverhay. Climb the narrow, wooded lane through Doverhay to a road junction (may not be signposted) and turn sharp ➜ to ascend **Crawter Hill**. Follow the narrow road into the next deep valley and climb to a T-junction, signposted Cloutsham and Stoke Pero.

**4** Descend into the next steep valley and carefully cross the ford (slippery, rocky and wet). Follow the road up to a car park with a scenic view. Turn ➜ at the car park and climb **Luccombe Hill**. Follow the road up and over the shoulder of **Dunkery Hill** and descend to the T-junction with the **B3224**. Turn ⬅ to the crossroads with the A396 in **Wheddon Cross** and turn ⬅ to follow the A396 through **Timberscombe** and back to **Dunster**.

## Link to Route 4

Please note that if you have linked Exe-Factor to Slam Dunk, there is no need to go all the way to Dunster. Turn ➜ at **Timberscombe** to rejoin Exe-Factor at the summit of **Exton Hill**.

# Route 6
*Blackdown Hills (Somerset and Devon)*

| | |
|---|---|
| **Start/Finish** | Blackbrook Pavilion car park, Taunton ST 247 239 |
| **Distance** | 76.5km (47½ miles) |
| **Ascent** | 1235m (4050ft) |
| **Grade** | |
| **Time** | 3hrs 30mins–4hrs 30mins |
| **Feed stations** | Boston Tea Party, Honiton; The King's Arms Inn, Stockland |
| **Access** | Exit the M5 at Junction 25 for Taunton onto the A358 and turn L at the first roundabout. Exit the dual carriageway at the next exit for Corfe and Taunton Racecourse, continue to a junction and turn L onto Ilminster Road. At the next roundabout turn R onto Blackbrook Way and, just before the next roundabout, turn L into the leisure centre car park. |

Tantalisingly close to the M5 motorway as drivers speed west, the high ridgeline of the Blackdown Hills is an area of Somerset and Devon that's something akin to a national treasure for local riders. With its sheer volume of cracking climbs and wiggling descents, you could ride up and down this compact training ground for several days without crossing the same quiet road twice; it's a beautiful area too. Although not overly long, this ride has its fair share of climbing: some gentle, some accumulative and some not subtle at all. But within this mixed bag of tricks comes some superb descending, especially right at the end – just when you think you've earned it.

## Overview

The high ground of the Blackdown Hills looms large over the Somerset levels and there's only one way to go – up. The initial climb from Taunton is challeng-ing but the Devon border opens up a terrific descent. The run into Honiton via Dunkeswell is relatively easy going, but the climb out is another story. Stockland and Chard are picked off soon enough, before crossing the A303 and beating one final tough climb leads to the final, rewarding descent.

**1** Turn ← out of the car park in **Taunton**, follow Blackbrook Way to a roundabout and turn ←. Continue along Chestnut Drive to the T-junction with the **B3170**. Turn ← over the **M5** to continue past the racecourse towards Corfe. Just before the White Hart Inn in **Corfe**, turn

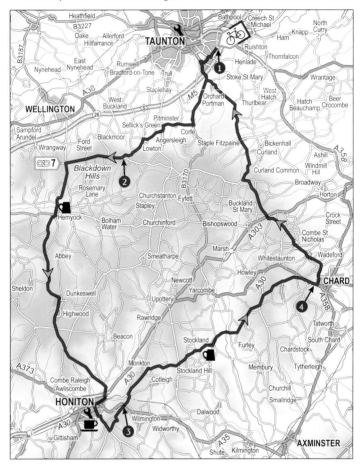

→ towards the village of Pitminster. Continue through **Pitminster** to a T-junction at **Sellick's Green** and turn ←. After 400m turn → onto Howleigh Lane towards Lowton and continue to a crossroads. Turn ← and climb to the T-junction at the summit of the hill.

**2** Turn → and follow the ridgeline road to the second crossroads.

Turn left at the pub in Hemyock

## Link to Route 7

To create a route that will test even the fittest riders, go ↑ into **Wellington** and follow A Ridge too Far, which will eventually return you to this same crossroads.

Turn ← into Devon and descend towards Hemyock. At the Catherine Wheel pub in **Hemyock**, turn ← towards Dunkeswell. Go past the airfield, through **Dunkeswell** and continue to a T-junction. Turn → and follow the road to the T-junction on the flyover adjacent to the **A30** at **Honiton**. Turn →, continue to a small roundabout

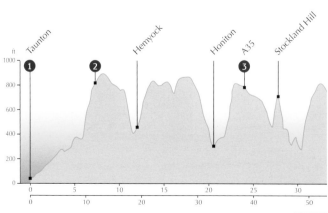

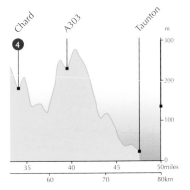

and then turn ➡ into Honiton High Street. Just past the large church with the memorial in front, turn ⬅ onto New Street and climb towards the station. Continue up past the hospital to a mini roundabout and turn ⬅ then immediately ➡ onto Lower Marlpits Hill. Go past the golf club at the summit and turn ⬅ towards the A35.

**3** Go ⬆, crossing the **A35**, to reach a T-junction and turn ➡ towards Cotleigh and Stockland. Follow the road past Cotleigh, climb **Stockland Hill** to a crossroads and go ⬆ to continue to Stockland village. Continue past the King's Arms Inn in **Stockland** and then turn ⬅ towards Yarcombe and Chard. Follow this lane over the River Yarty to a staggered junction and turn ⬅ towards Chard to reach a T-junction on the **A30**. Turn ➡ and descend into Chard High Street.

**4** On entering **Chard**, turn ⬅ beside an old flint wall onto Helliers Road towards Wadeford and Combe St Nicholas. Continue through **Combe St Nicholas** to the staggered road junction on the **A303** and go ⬆. Continue to climb steadily to a road junction at the summit and turn ➡ to descend towards Staple Fitzpaine and Orchard

Turn right for the final descent towards Taunton

Portman. At the T-junction with the **B3170**, turn ➡ over the **M5** back into **Taunton** and immediately turn ➡ onto Chestnut Drive. At the roundabout turn ➡ onto Blackbrook Way and return to the car park.

# Route 7
## *A Ridge too Far (Somerset)*

| | |
|---|---|
| **Start/Finish** | Wellington Sports Centre, Wellington ST 131 208 |
| **Distance** | 105.5km (65½ miles) |
| **Ascent** | 1600m (5250ft) |
| **Grade** | |
| **Time** | 4hrs 30mins–6hrs |
| **Feed stations** | Raleghs Cross Inn, Brendon Hill; Pines Café, Buncombe Hill |
| **Access** | Exit the M5 at Junction 26 and follow road signs into the centre of Wellington. At the staggered junction in the town centre, turn R onto North Street (B3187) and follow the brown tourist signs for the leisure centre, which is situated at the end of Corams Lane. |

As tough as it is beautiful, this corner of Somerset includes all the ingredients for a classic day in the saddle: quiet country roads, decent surfaces, stunning countryside, dramatic views, wicked descents and a hill climb that leaves you feeling like you're King of the Mountains.

## Overview

A steady warm up out of Wellington leads to the start of the hills around Wiveliscombe and from here the contours begin to squeeze up close and muscles soon tighten. Balancing out this effort is a stunning descent to the coast at Watchet and a chance to recover (only slightly) before the wall of the Quantock Hills poses a real threat to tired legs. After ricocheting off Bridgwater, plenty of flat (ish) riding paves the way for the long, tough climb to the Pines Café at the summit of Buncombe Hill. It's then all downhill to Taunton but the distant spike of the Wellington Memorial high up on the Blackdown Hills is a constant reminder to keep something in reserve; otherwise it might just be a ridge too far for some.

 Leave the car park in **Wellington** by the way you came in and return to the **B3187**. Turn ←, continue to the roundabout just beyond **Milverton** and then turn ← onto the **B3227** towards Wiveliscombe. At the traffic lights at the crossroads in **Wiveliscombe** turn → onto High Street and continue into the town square. Turn → here onto North Street, continue for 1.5km to **Langley** and turn → towards Whitefield and Raleighs Cross. Follow the lane as it peaks and troughs to the **B3224**, then turn ← for 1.3km to **Raleighs Cross**.

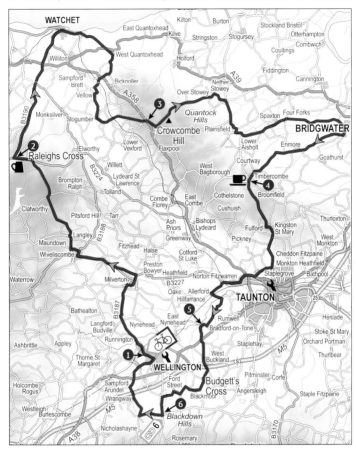

**2**    Turn → opposite the Ralegh's Cross Inn onto the **B3190** towards Watchet and descend to the crossroads on the **A39**. Go ↑ towards Watchet and remain on this road as it passes the railway station. Continue out through **Watchet** on Doniford Road to the crossroads on the **A39**. Go ↑ towards **West Quantoxhead** to the Staple Cross T-junction, and turn → towards Bicknoller. Follow the road to the **A358** and go ↑ towards Vellow and

Stogumber. At the crossroads in **Stogumber**, turn ← onto Station Road and continue to the **A358**.

**③** Go ↑ into Crowcombe and, just past the church, turn ← up **Crowcombe Hill** towards Over Stowey and Nether Stowey. After the summit, descend to a triangular junction and turn → towards Nether Stowey and Bridgwater. Continue to a crossroads and turn →. Follow the road towards Plainsfield and Taunton then, as the road sweeps down towards Hawkridge Reservoir, turn sharp ← towards Spaxton and Bridgwater. Continue to the edge of **Bridgwater** and turn → towards Enmore, Bishops Lydeard and Taunton. Circle Durleigh Reservoir towards **Enmore** and continue to the Pines Café just beyond the summit of the long climb at **Timbercombe**.

**④** Turn ← at the crossroads opposite the Pines Café and descend towards Kingston St Mary and Taunton. On reaching a small crossroads on the outskirts of **Taunton**, turn → just before the traffic lights onto Corkscrew Lane. Follow the lane to the T-junction with the **A358** and turn →. Go ↑ at the first roundabout, then turn ← at the next roundabout onto the **B3227** towards Norton Fitzwarren. On exiting **Norton Fitzwarren**, turn ← immediately after the railway bridge towards Allerford. Continue to the next road junction and turn ← towards Bradford-on-Tone.

At Staple Cross, turn right for Bicknoller

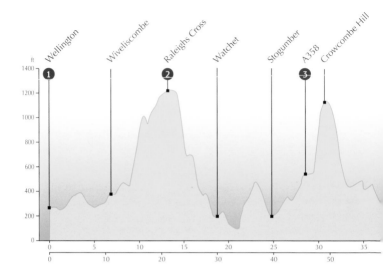

Turn right onto Taunton's Corkscrew Lane for a flat recovery section

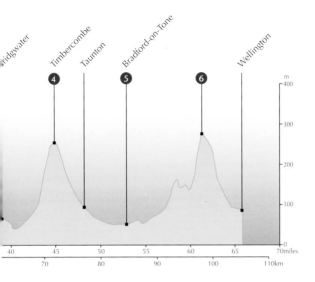

**5** Continue through **Bradford-on-Tone** to the **A38** and go ⬆, through **West Buckland** and over the **M5**. Go through **Budgett's Cross** to the hamlet of **Blackmoor**. Turn ➡ just as the road rises on a ↰ bend and continue to a small grass triangle, and then turn ⬅ to a T-junction at **Ford Street**. Turn ➡ and then ⬅ onto a narrow lane opposite a large white cottage and continue to a small crossroads. Turn ⬅ and climb towards the Wellington Memorial on the ridgeline.

## Link to Route 6
Can't get enough? Go ⬆ at the crossroads at the summit to join Blackdown Hills for an even more memorable day in the saddle.

**6** At the crossroads at the summit, turn ➡ to go past the Wellington Memorial and descend towards **Wrangway**. Go over the **M5** to a cross-roads, turn ➡ and continue to the **A38**. Turn ➡ then immediately ⬅ onto Bagley Road and continue to a T-junction. Turn ➡, follow the road into the centre of **Wellington** and turn ⬅ onto the **B3187**. Follow the signs for the leisure centre to return to the car park.

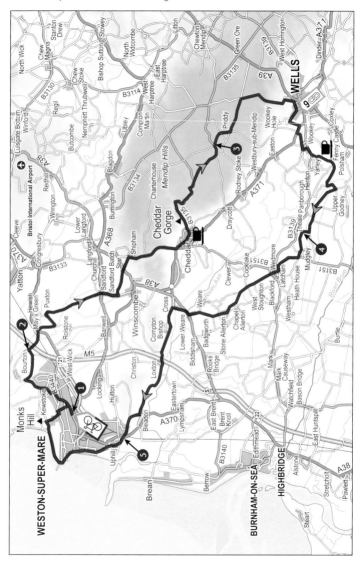

# Route 8
*Weston-super-Nightmare (Somerset)*

| | |
|---|---|
| **Start/Finish** | Hutton Moor Leisure Centre, Weston-super-Mare ST 340 611 |
| **Distance** | 89.75km (53¾ miles) |
| **Ascent** | 880m (2885ft) |
| **Grade** | |
| **Time** | 3hrs 30mins–5hrs |
| **Feed stations** | Costa Coffee, Cheddar Gorge; Fenny Castle Tea Rooms, near Wookey |
| **Access** | Exit the M5 at Junction 21 and follow the A370 dual carriageway towards the town centre. Just after the third roundabout on the dual carriageway, turn R for the leisure centre. |

Once you've wormed your way out of Weston-super-Mare, you're in for a real treat: the Mendip Hills play host to a cracking sportive that, although not particularly steep, still includes one of the most dramatic and famous hill climbs in the south west of England. Of course, the descent from the top into Wells is a cracker too. The lovely and warm Fenny Castle Tea Rooms allows riders to recuperate within the Somerset Levels, but beguiles unwary riders into a false sense of security, as the contours soon tighten up quite unexpectedly. And if you were wondering where the nightmare element to this ride is? Just wait until you've cruised idly past the sea front at Weston-super-Mare.

## Overview
The open levels of Somerset provide riders with the chance to get fresh legs spinning and plenty of mileage on the clock. But all too soon after leaving Weston-super-Mare, the Mendip Hills appear in front of you, and you know things are going to change. After a few leg stretching climbs towards Shipham, the road descends rapidly into Cheddar before you take on the dramatic ascent up through the famous Cheddar Gorge – this is as good as climbing gets. With the fast descent into Wells on which to recover, the levels beckon again to provide welcome respite. Towards the finish, however, the contours once again make their presence felt before the final challenge of Monks Hill appears – you have been warned!

 Exit ← from the leisure centre car park in **Weston-super-Mare**, follow the road over the railway to the T-junction with the **B3440** and turn →.

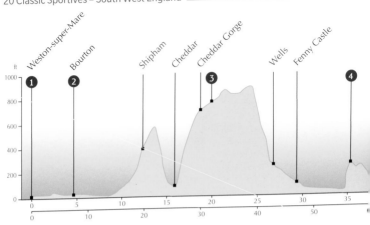

Go ⬆ at the roundabout next to the recreation ground to reach the junction just before the petrol station and turn ⬅ onto Milton Road, then immediately ➡ into Worle High Street. Turn ⬅ at the mini roundabout in the centre of Worle, continue to a small grass triangle and turn ➡ onto Hollow Lane. At the bottom of the short descent turn ⬅ onto Ebdon Road. Follow this road over two mini roundabouts, keeping open countryside to your left, to reach the T-junction with Ebdon Lane. Turn ➡ towards Bourton.

**2** At the T-junction in **Bourton** turn ➡ and go over the **M5** to the junction with the **A370**. Turn ➡ then immediately ⬅ for May's Green and Puxton. Continue to a T-junction and turn ⬅. Continue through **Puxton** to the **A368** in **Sandford** and go ⬆ to climb Hill Road into **Sandford Batch**. Turn ⬅ onto Shipham Lane opposite the entrance to the cemetery and continue to the A38 in **Star**. Go ⬆ at the **A38** to the crossroads in **Shipham** and turn ➡. Follow this road to the roundabout beside the A371 but turn ⬅ to keep the petrol station on your ↱ side (this is the **B3135**) and continue to the mini roundabout in **Cheddar**. Turn ⬅ and climb the B3135 up through **Cheddar Gorge**. As you near the summit of this long climb, turn ➡ for Priddy.

**3** Continue through **Priddy** to the crossroads, turn ➡ beside the old coaching inn and descend into Wells.

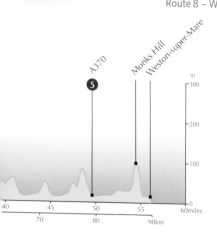

## Link to Route 9

To link this ride to Mid-Somer Murder, turn ← at the T-junction at the bottom of the hill onto the **A39**. Turn → and follow the A39 through **Wells**.

At the T-junction at the bottom of the hill turn → onto Ash Lane. Follow it out of **Wells** to a sharp ↱ bend on a rise, and turn ← onto Glencot Road for Haybridge. At the T-junction with the **A371** turn → then, at the next crossroads, turn ← into **Wookey**. Continue through the village to the **B3139** and turn →. After 300m turn ← for Fenny Castle, and continue to a small crossroads amid the ditches, signposted Panborough. Turn → and continue to another crossroads. Go ↑ here until the high ridgeline appears across to the right. At the second road junction turn → onto Dagg's Lane and climb to a T-junction.

At the triangle, turn right onto Hollow Lane

Monks Hill: let the nightmare begin

**4** Turn ← and follow Snake Lane to the **B3151** and turn → to descend into Latcham. At the staggered junction in the centre of **Latcham**, turn ← then, at the mini roundabout, turn → and continue to a T-junction opposite the church. Turn ←, then turn next → for Stoughton and Weare. Follow the lane past the windmill to the **A38** at **Lower Weare**. Turn → onto the A38, then turn ← for Cross. At the T-junction in **Cross** turn ← and continue over the **M5** into Loxton. On entering **Loxton**, turn ← onto Shiplate Road and continue to Bleadon. At the sharp ↰ corner in **Bleadon** turn → uphill onto Celtic Way and continue to the **A370**.

**5** Go ↑ at the A370 to the roundabout and turn ← onto Uphill Road. Continue along this road to the A370 again and turn ← to go along the promenade at **Weston-super-Mare**. Go past the pier and follow the coast road around the headland along Birnbeck Road. With the steep woodland on your right and the coast on your left continue into **Kewstoke** and turn → up **Monks Hill**. At the summit follow the road down to a road junction and turn → then immediately ← onto Baytree Road. At the traffic lights go ↑ to a roundabout and turn → onto the **B3440**. Take the next turning ← onto Locking Moor Road and go over the railway to the roundabout. In the right-hand corner, before going onto the roundabout, turn → onto the cyclepath that runs parallel to the dual carriageway. Follow the cyclepath back to the leisure centre.

# Route 9
*Mid-Somer Murder (Somerset)*

| | |
|---|---|
| **Start/Finish** | Wells Leisure Centre, Wells ST 536 461 |
| **Distance** | 87.75km (54½ miles) |
| **Ascent** | 850m (2790ft) |
| **Grade** | ▲▲ |
| **Time** | 3hrs 30mins–5hrs |
| **Feed stations** | Truffles Brasserie, Bruton; The George Inn, Nunney |
| **Access** | Follow the A371 to the traffic lights in the centre of Wells, then follow the brown tourist signs for the leisure centre and rugby club into Charter Way. The leisure centre is near the end of the road. |

The best way to describe the area of the Somerset Levels around Wells and Glastonbury is pancake-flat, but Mid-Somer Murder has an element of Jekyll and Hyde about it. With a westerly tailwind, you'll quickly eat up the early miles but, beyond Bruton, the terrain takes on a different feel: the hills get longer, trees reappear and a magical castle pops up out of nowhere!

## Overview

Following the quick initial section out of Wells and stopping off for a brew in Bruton, the long, steady climb up Gare Hill is a welcoming leg-stretch to combat the lack of testing contours. After bouncing off the western edge of Frome, the high ground of Old Wells Road beyond Mells offers far-reaching Somerset Levels views and easy pedalling, before a long super-swift descent back into Wells brings proceedings to a dramatic close. The iconic mound of Glastonbury Tor is never far from view and acts like a navigational beacon on both the run out and the run home.

**1** Turn ➡ out of the car park in **Wells** to a T-junction, turn ⬅ and continue up to the T-junction with the **A371**. Turn ⬅ and continue down to the traffic lights. Turn ➡ onto the **A39** and, at the next roundabout, turn ⬅ to follow the A39. Just after leaving Wells turn ⬅ onto Woodford Lane and continue to the crossroads in **Launcherley**. Turn ➡ before the farm, where the road drops away. At the next road junction turn ➡ (Glastonbury Tor should be within sight here) and follow the straight and narrow lane to the T-junction with the **A39**. Turn ⬅ and follow the cyclepath to the roundabout.

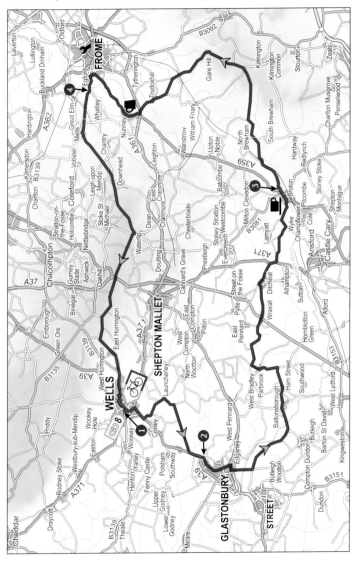

Glastonbury Tor dominates the skyline for miles

**2** Turn ← at the roundabout for Glastonbury, follow the road across the top of the High Street and continue to the mini roundabout on the A361. Turn →, then turn ← onto Butleigh Old Road to a T-junction and turn ←. Follow the road over Cow Bridge to the crossroads and turn ← for Baltonsborough. Go ↑ at the staggered crossroads in **Baltonsborough**, continue through Ham Street to a T-junction and turn ← into **Parbrook**. Take the second junction in Parbrook onto Parbrook Lane, climb to a crossroads and turn → to continue to the **A37** at **Wraxall**. Go ↑ at the A37 and continue through **Ditcheat** to the T-junction with the **A371**. Turn → then take the next ← for Wyke Champflower and Bruton. At the T-junction in **Bruton**, turn ← (Truffles Brasserie is immediately on your left) through the High Street to a T-junction and turn ← to carry straight on. As the road climbs out of Bruton, turn → at the sharp ↰ bend for North Brewham.

**3** Continue through **North Brewham** and up the long wooded climb of **Gare Hill**. After recovering on the plateau of the summit, turn ← at the sharp ↦ corner to go over the railway line, then continue through Trudoxhill to the **A361**. Turn ←, take the third exit off the roundabout into **Nunney** and go past the castle to continue towards Frome. Just beyond Frome Golf Club, turn ← at the crossroads onto Oakfield Road and continue to a T-junction in **Frome**. Turn ← and descend into **Egford**, cross Nunney Brook and turn → (may not be signposted!) to go through the woods at Murder Combe.

Stay on the brakes and turn left

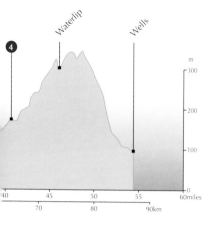

**4** After a long and flat road section, keep your speed down as you descend towards some cottages in **Mells** to take the sharp ← turn at the crossroads, for Mells Green and Wells. Climb gently to a T-junction and turn → onto Old Wells Road to the T-junction at **Waterlip**. Turn → then immediately ← to follow the high ground to the **A37**. Go ↑ at the A37 to descend through **East Horrington** to the **B3139**. Turn ←, continue to a T-junction near the cathedral in **Wells** and turn →. Continue to a mini roundabout and turn →, then turn ← at the traffic lights. Go ↑ at the next lights, following signs for the A371 (Weston-super-Mare) and go up the hill.

## Link to Route 8
Carry on along the **A371** for 1km then turn ← onto the **B3139** for 2km. Turn ← for **Fenny Castle** to join Weston-super-Nightmare.

Continue up the hill then turn → onto Charter Way to return to the leisure centre.

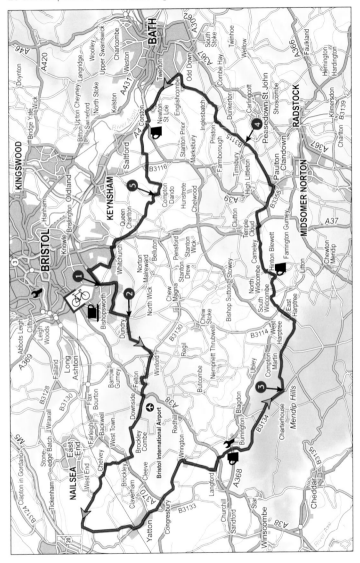

# Route 10
*Mendip Madness (Somerset)*

| | |
|---|---|
| **Start/Finish** | Hengrove Park Leisure Complex, Bristol ST 593 688 |
| **Distance** | 90km (56 miles) |
| **Ascent** | 1270m (4165ft) |
| **Grade** | |
| **Time** | 4hrs–5hrs 30mins |
| **Feed stations** | Burrington Inn, Burrington Combe; Ring O'Bells, Hinton Blewett; The Globe, Newton St Loe |
| **Access** | Hengrove Leisure Park is found on the southern tip of the City of Bristol, with easy access from several junctions from the M5 to the west, or by following signs for Bristol Airport from the A37 and the A4 to the east. The leisure centre is just off the large roundabout on the A4174, between Airport Road and the A37. |

The southern edge of Bristol is home to this eclectic, challenging ride over the Mendip Hills and, soon after you start, you'll be climbing high above the city and cruising down one of the route's many superb descents. Burrington Combe hosts a bike shop, a warm café and the start of a classic hill climb all in the space of a few metres – sportive rides simply don't come better equipped than this. Although the descending is fun and plentiful, the numerous hills leave little time for recovery. You'll need to work hard and dig a little deeper on some of the climbs, especially around the edge of Bath and beyond.

## Overview

The introductory climb from Bristol towards Dundry is a classic in itself – hairpin bends and all. If the climbing is challenging then the descending is almost perfect, as the fast-rolling tarmac of Brockley Combe quickly leaves Bristol Airport in its wake. With a touch of the Somerset levels near Nailsea and Yatton on which to compose yourself, the classic ascent of Burrington Combe can be attacked with the heart and lungs of a mountain goat. With Hinton Blewett, Englishcombe, Corston and Compton Dando all having hills that will happily leave their mark on any unprepared rider, there are plenty more ups and downs before reaching the finish line.

**1** Exit the leisure complex car park, turn ← and follow the cyclepath alongside the dual carriageway to a large roundabout. Follow the cyclepath into the subway and into the centre of the roundabout, then take the cycle route exit onto Hawkfield Road towards Hartcliffe. Follow the road for 1km then, opposite a blocks of flats, turn ← onto Bishport Avenue and continue to the T-junction with Queen's Road. Turn ← and climb to the summit. At the top of the climb, carefully turn → onto West Dundry Lane.

**2** Continue along the lane and descend to the T-junction with the **B3130** in **Winford**. Turn → then immediately ← onto Felton Lane and continue to the T-junction on the **A38**. Turn ← and then, just before the foot-bridge, carefully turn → onto Downside Road and the Avon Cycleway. Continue past the **airport**, descend through **Brockley Combe** to the **A370** and go ↑. Follow the Avon Cycleway to a T-junction, turn ← onto Chelvey Road and go over the railway line to the next T-junction. Turn ←, continue to the small grassy triangle adjacent to the River Kenn and turn ← towards Yatton. At the T-junction with the **B3133**, turn ← through **Yatton** and, just after the entrance to the large hotel, turn ← onto the narrow lane towards the A370 and Wrington. Go ↑ at the **A370**, continue through **Wrington** to a T-junction in **Langford** and turn ← to the A38. Go ↑ at the **A38** and continue to the junction with the **A368**. Turn → then immediately ← onto the **B3134** to climb Burrington Combe.

**3** At the top of the long climb, turn ← just after the old filling station and follow NCN Route 3 to descend to a crossroads. Go ↑ to continue

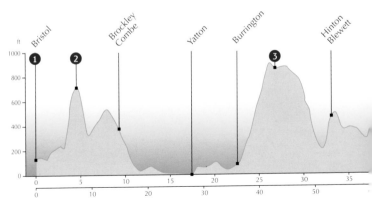

Turn left at the River Kenn towards Yatton

descending to the **B3114** in **East Harptree**. Go ↑ to follow the cycle route, turn → at **South Widcombe** and climb to **Hinton Blewett**. Just after the Ring O'Bells pub, turn → for Cameley and continue to the **A37** at **Temple Cloud**. Turn → then immediately ← onto a narrow lane, continue to a T-junction and turn → for the A39. Turn ← then immediately → onto the **B3355** for Paulton. Go ↑ at the roundabout in **Paulton** to a mini roundabout, turn ← onto the High Street and continue up to the **B3115**.

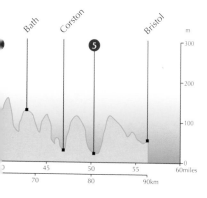

Ashton Hill – a very cheeky climb

**4** Turn → and climb to the top of the hill. At the summit, turn ← onto a narrow lane and descend into **Priston**. Turn → at the triangle in the village and follow the road through **Englishcombe** to a T-junction on the edge of **Bath**. Turn ← and continue to the roundabout with the A39/A4. Turn ← onto the **A39** into **Corston** and turn → up the steep climb of Ashton Hill. Continue to a crossroads and turn ←, then turn → to the **B3116** and carefully go ↑ to descend into **Compton Dando**. At the T-junction in the village turn →, go over the river and turn ← onto Peppershells Lane.

**5** At the summit go ↑ at the crossroads to a T-junction and turn → onto Woollard Lane. Follow the road to a sharp ↰ turn just before the A37 and turn → onto Sleep Lane for Whitchurch and Bristol. Continue to a mini roundabout and turn ← to the **A37**. Turn → for 200m then, oppo-site the chapel, turn ← onto Maggs Lane. At the end of the lane turn → then immediately ← onto Whitchurch Lane. Continue through a housing estate in **Bristol**, turn → onto Bamfield and continue to traffic lights. Turn ← onto the cyclepath to return to the car park at Hengrove Park.

# Route 11
*Over the Edge (Gloucestershire)*

| | |
|---|---|
| **Start/Finish** | Yate Leisure Centre, Yate ST 713 825 |
| **Distance** | 101.5km (63 miles) |
| **Ascent** | 1335m (4380ft) |
| **Grade** | |
| **Time** | 4hrs–5hrs 30mins |
| **Feed stations** | The Berkeley Arms, Tites Point (detour); Berry Blue Café, Lower Cam; The George Inn, Frocester; The Bear of Rodborough Hotel, Rodborough Common; Rose & Crown, Nympsfield |
| **Access** | Exit the M4 at Junction 18 and follow signs for Chipping Sodbury, via the A46 and the A432 (Kennedy Way). As Chipping Sodbury morphs into Yate, the leisure centre can be found beside the roundabout where Kennedy Way and Station Road converge. |

Just a stone's throw from the heart of Bristol, Yate is the launch pad for a spectacular sportive alongside the Severn Estuary. The contours of this ride refuse to go away until the last few miles, so keep something in reserve, even if it's just a Mars bar.

## Overview

The contours may be scarce on the ground at the start, but the cadence-perfect opening flat section of this ride out from Yate is not short on dramatic scenery or excellent road surfaces. The view across the Bristol Channel around Thornbury is superb, as are the fast-flowing road sections that hungrily speed you towards the hills beyond Dursley. Short and steep climbs then feed long and sweeping descents that leave you howling like a wolf, but beware Bear Hill at Woodchester; it'll squeeze the last remaining breath from your lungs if you attack too fast. The subsequent long descent into Wotton-under-Edge is one of the highlights of this ride: super smooth and wiggly enough for a touch of alpine descending, it's just the ticket for the start of the return journey back to Yate.

**1** Exit the car park in **Yate** and turn → then, at the roundabout, turn ← and take the second exit off the next roundabout onto the **A432**. As you rise over the railway line turn → onto North Road to a crossroads and go ↑. Continue to the T-junction with the **B4058** and turn →.

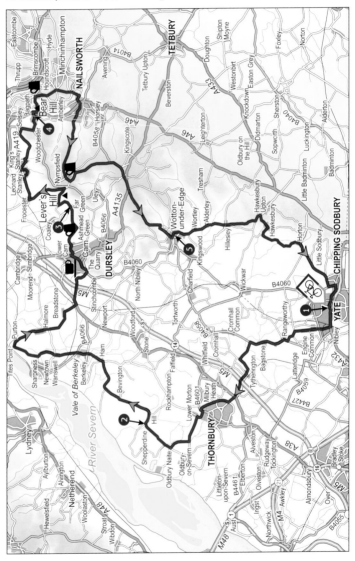

After Thornbury turn right onto The Naite

Follow the road through **Rangeworthy** and **Bagstone** then turn ← for Tytherington. Go over the **M5** to the **A38** and turn ← then immediately → to a roundabout at **Thornbury**. Turn →, continue to the **B4061** and turn ← then immediately → towards Oldbury-on-Severn. At the cross-roads at **Oldbury Naite**, turn → onto NCN Route 41 along The Naite and continue to a T-junction.

**2** Turn →, follow the road through **Hill** to the T-junction at **Ham** and turn ←. At the T-junction in **Berkeley** turn ← then immediately → to a roundabout. Go ↑ and follow the road through **Wanswell** to a sharp ↰ corner and turn → for Purton. (It's worth a quick detour here to see if the pub at **Tites Point** is open. Turn ← over the canal in **Purton** and continue to the end of the lane.) Turn → to a T-junction and turn ← to continue to the **A38**. Turn ← then turn → onto the **B4066** and go over the **M5** towards Cam. Turn ← at the T-junction with the **B4060**, and then turn ← again onto Woodfield Road to the roundabout on the **A4135**. Turn ← towards Lower Cam. At the next roundabout turn → (café stop on your left) to a small rise in the road just beyond the Railway Inn, and turn ← onto Upthorpe. Continue to the T-junction in **Ashmead Green** and turn ← towards Coaley.

**3** At the junction on the sharp ↰ turn in **Far Green**, turn → towards Uley, and then turn immediately ← onto The Ham. Just beyond Ham Farm turn → at the tiny grass island to climb **Lever's Hill**.

## Shortcut to Nympsfield

If you're having a bad day and need a shortcut, turn → at the top of Lever's Hill to the **B4066** and go ↑ to rejoin the route at **Nympsfield**.

At the T-junction at the top turn ← and descend Frocester Hill into **Frocester**. At the junction opposite the George Inn, turn → to go through **Leonard Stanley** and into **King's Stanley**. Follow the road into the High Street in the village and turn → at the mini roundabout beside the King's Head pub towards Selsley and Woodchester. As you climb into **Selsley**, turn → onto Selsley Common, sign-posted Woodchester. At the T-junction with the **B4066** turn →, and then turn ← over a cattle grid to descend into **Woodchester**.

**4** At the bottom, turn → onto the **A46** and then turn ← onto **Bear Hill**. At the T-junction at the summit turn →. Go past the The Bear of Rodborough Hotel and onto Minchinhampton Common to reach a staggered crossroads, and turn → to descend The Ladder into Nailsworth. At the crossroads with the **A46** in **Nailsworth**, go ↑ to climb Spring Hill and continue to Nympsfield. Go ↑ at the crossroads in **Nympsfield** to a T-junction and turn ←. Follow the road to the T-junction with the **A4135**. Turn →, then turn ← to join the **B4058** and descend to the roundabout in **Wotton-under-Edge**.

**5** Turn ← at the junction beside the memorial, then take the second turning → onto School Road and follow this road out through **Wortley** and **Hillesley**. Just past the impressive Lord Somerset Monument at

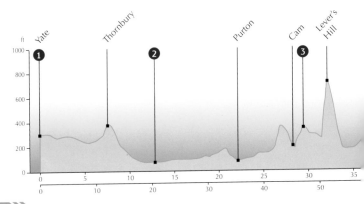

Procester: turn right for Leonard Stanley

**Hawkesbury Upton**, turn ➡ to descend into **Hawkesbury** and reach a T-junction. Turn ⬅, follow the lane to the T-junction in **Horton** and turn ➡ to continue to the T-junction on the edge of Chipping Sodbury. Turn ➡ and continue to a roundabout. Turn ⬅ and go ⬆ at a mini roundabout to the High Street in **Chipping Sodbury** and turn ➡. Go ⬆ at two roundabouts to a third roundabout, in **Yate**, and turn ⬅ to return to the leisure centre car park on your left.

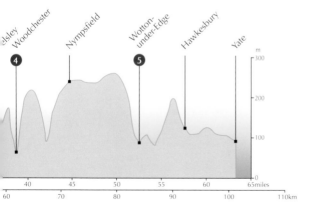

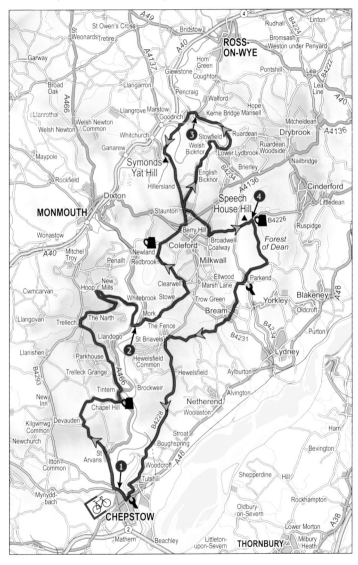

# Route 12
*Forest of Dean (Gloucestershire)*

| | |
|---|---|
| **Start/Finish** | Chepstow Leisure Centre, Chepstow ST 526 945 |
| **Distance** | 93.25km (58 miles) |
| **Ascent** | 1590m (5215ft) |
| **Grade** | ▲▲▲ |
| **Time** | 4hrs–5hrs 30mins |
| **Feed stations** | Royal George Hotel, Tintern; The Ostrich Inn, Newland; The Speech House Hotel, Speech Hill |
| **Access** | Exit the M48 at Junction 2 for Chepstow, follow the A466 to a large roundabout and go SA to continue on the A466. At the next large roundabout turn R onto the B4293 (Welsh Street). After around 300m, the leisure centre is found on the left. |

The route starts in Wales, not South West England, granted, but the Wye Valley and the Forest of Dean together comprise an area that refutes boundaries to become the perfect playground for sportive training. This pretty-as-a-picture figure-of-eight route encompasses enough challenging terrain to keep the most ardent of riders puffing. Long climbs precede superb descents, but don't be fooled; the beguiling terrain of the Forest of Dean will turn lean legs into jellied eels for unwary riders.

## Overview
Tintern and the meanderings of the River Wye are hard to leave behind following the initial section out of Chepstow, but the climb up to Trellech calls like a siren to riders, and the descending thereafter is superb. Symonds Yat Hill demands respect, but don't underestimate Speech House Hill either; it will try hard to catch you out. With the hardest climbing behind you, the rush back into Chepstow is a real treat: the excellent surface and sweeping corners keep the momentum turning right to the final crossing over the river and back into Wales.

**1** Exit ➡ from the car park in **Chepstow**, continue to the roundabout and take the third exit onto the **A466**. Go past the racecourse to the ➡ corner in **St Arvans** and turn ⬅ onto Devauden Road. Climb gently to the summit and turn ➡ for Tintern. At the T-junction with the A466, turn ⬅ to continue to Tintern Parva. Turn ⬅ by the Wye Valley Hotel onto Trellech Road to climb to the **B4293** at **Trellech**. Turn ➡ then ➡ again at the sharp ← corner towards The Narth. Follow the road through **The Narth** to a crossroads near **Hoop**, and turn → to descend through **Whitebrook** to the T-junction with the A466.

**2** Turn ← across the River Wye and turn immediately → to climb into Gloucestershire and up through **Mork**. At the next T-junction, turn ← towards Clearwell and Newland. Just beyond the Ostrich Inn in **Newland**, turn → to the crossroads with the B4228 and go ↑ to the **A4136**. Turn → to the crossroads and turn ←. Follow the road through **English Bicknor** and **Stowfield** to the B4234 and turn ←. Follow the River Wye to where the road narrows and turn ← onto the B4229 for Goodrich.

**3** Just beyond **Goodrich**, turn ← over the river for Symonds Yat and climb **Symonds Yat Hill** up to **Hillersland** to reach a T-junction. Turn → then immediately ← onto Park Road and continue to the **A4136**. Go ↑ onto the B4432 to a crossroads, go ↑ through **Broadwell** to another cross-roads and turn ← onto the **B4226**. Descend then climb **Speech House Hill** to the hotel at the summit.

**4** Turn → at the hotel and descend to a T-junction. Turn → through **Parkend** to a toll house with a green door and turn ← for Bream and St Briavels. At the T-junction with the **B4231** in **Bream**, turn → then immediately ← onto Parawell Lane, and continue to the crossroads in

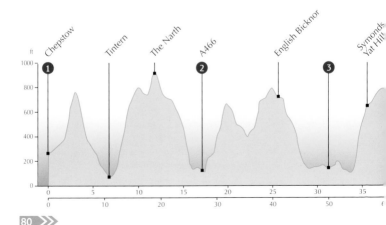

Turning left for Bream

St Briavels. Turn ← and follow the **B4228** to the double mini roundabout in **Tutshill**. Turn → onto Castleford Hill and descend to the bridge. Cross the river into **Chepstow** and follow the one-way circuit into the town centre. Turn ← onto the High Street, continue through the narrow archway and turn → onto Welsh Street (B4293). Climb to the leisure centre car park and turn →.

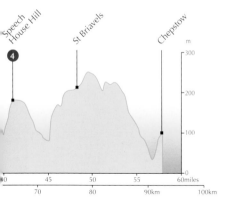

# Route 13
*Cotswold Caper (Cotswolds)*

| | |
|---|---|
| **Start/Finish** | Cotswold Leisure Centre, Cirencester SP 019 018 |
| **Distance** | 108km (67 miles) |
| **Ascent** | 1425m (4675ft) |
| **Grade** | |
| **Time** | 4hrs 30mins–6hrs |
| **Feed stations** | The White Hart Inn, Winchcombe; The Old Post Office, Guiting Power; The Chestnut Tree, Bourton-on-the-Water |
| **Access** | Exit the A417 for Cirencester, follow the A429 to a roundabout and go SA to follow London Road to a T-junction, then turn R onto Sheep Street. Cotswold Leisure Centre can be found on Tetbury Road, which is behind the large Waitrose store. |

If it were a Disney film, Cotswold Caper would be **Beauty and the Beast**. The gruelling climb of Bushcombe Lane out of Bishop's Cleeve is a beastly ascent, but every other hill is a cinch in comparison. Beyond Winchcombe, beautiful honey-coloured Cotswold villages pepper the route, where plenty of pubs and cafés provide excellent watering holes. You'll have every right to feel pleased with yourself at the end of this ride. It's challenging, for sure, but it's great fun too.

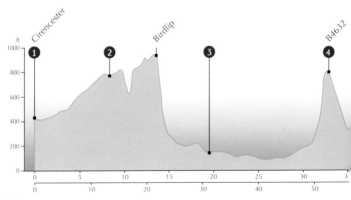

## Overview

The run north from historic Cirencester hides no horrors as it crosses easy-on-the-eye and easy-on-the-pedal terrain, squeezing in-between Gloucester and Cheltenham. Even big hills like Birdlip are descended rather than climbed. But that all changes at Bishop's Cleeve, as Bushcombe Lane (especially when wet) lives up to its reputation as one of the toughest climbs in England's south west. Winchcombe brings welcome respite in both descending and warm tea and toast, but it's back to work soon after as Round Hill stretches the sinews. Gentle contours continue through the rest of the route, right up to the maze of streets that aims to confound you on your return to Cirencester.

**1** Exit the leisure centre car park in **Cirencester**, turn ➡ onto Tetbury Road and then keep ⬅ onto Park Lane. Turn ⬅ again onto Park Street, which unfolds into Thomas Street. At a T-junction turn ⬅ then ➡ to follow Spitalgate Lane to a crossroads, and turn ⬅ onto the A417. Continue on the road as it carries straight on along Gloucester Road through **Stratton**, and turn ⬅ towards **Daglingworth** to continue to a T-junction. Turn ➡ and follow the road towards Winstone. Turn ⬅ just before Winstone, towards Caudle Green and Brimpsfield.

**2** Descend and then climb up to **Brimpsfield**, and continue to the **B4070** at **Birdlip**. Turn ⬅ and then turn ➡ at the sharp ⬅ bend to descend **Birdlip Hill**. At the roundabout on the **A46** go ⬆ then, shortly afterwards, turn ➡ just before the large brown flats onto Vicarage Lane.

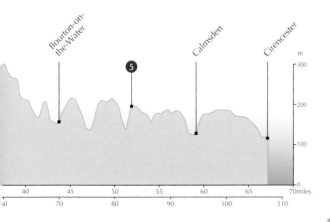

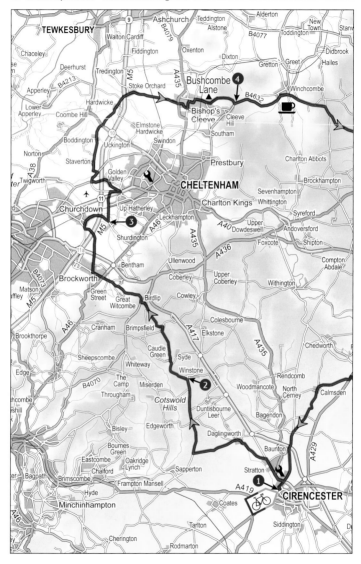

Bushcombe Lane: where the Devil rides out

At the mini roundabout turn ← and at the next roundabout turn →
onto Court Road. Continue over the **A417** and the **M5** to a T-junction
and turn → into **Churchdown**. Continue to a mini roundabout, go ↑
and turn → onto Station Road. Continue to a mini roundabout and
turn → onto Church Road. At the next mini roundabout, turn ← onto
Brookfield Road. Continue over the **M5** to a T-junction and turn ← onto
Badgeworth Road.

**3** Follow the road under the **A40** to the B4063, turn ← to go under the
**M5** to the traffic lights at a crossroads and turn → onto the B4634. As
the road rises to go back over the M5, turn ← for Staverton and continue to the T-junction with the A4019. Turn →, and then turn ← beside
the Gloucester Old Spot pub for Stoke Orchard and Bishop's Cleeve.
Go ↑ at the roundabout in **Bishop's Cleeve** to a crossroads, turn ←
onto Cheltenham Road and continue to a mini roundabout. Turn →,
continue to the next roundabout and take the second exit to go along
Church Road. Continue to a T-junction and turn → along Station Road.
Go under the railway bridge, continue for 400m and turn ← to climb
Bushcombe Lane (enjoy!). At the T-junction with the **B4632**, turn ←.

**4** Descend the long hill into **Winchcombe**, turn → just after the
Methodist chapel onto Castle Street and climb **Round Hill** to continue

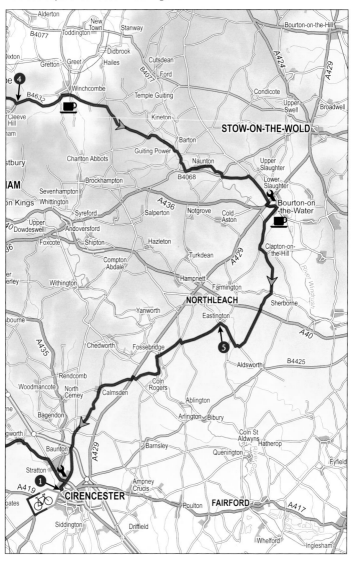

Picturesque Bourton-on-the-Water

to **Guiting Power**. Just beyond Guiting Power, turn → to go over the River Windrush and turn ← to climb to the B4068. Turn ← then immediately ← again to go through **Naunton** to the **B4068**. Go ↑ at the crossroads, continue up to another crossroads and turn →. Continue to the **A429** and turn → then immediately ← into **Bourton-on-the-Water**. At the crossroads in the centre of the village turn → onto Sherborne Street, and follow this lane all the way to the A40. Go ↑ at the **A40** to a T-junction, turn → and continue to a grass triangular junction. Turn ← for Fossebridge.

**5** At the next junction turn →, then turn ← to descend into **Coln St Dennis**. Follow the road around the back of the church to continue to **Coln Rogers**. At the road junction in the hamlet turn → to follow NCN Route 48 to the **A429**. Turn ← and then immediately → to continue on NCN Route 48. Continue into **Calmsden**, turn ← to continue along NCN Route 48 and continue to a T-junction. Turn ← and go over the dual carriageway, following The Whiteway to the **A417**. Go ↑, follow Spitalgate Lane around the one-way system to the market place in **Cirencester** and turn → onto Castle Street. Turn →, continue to a roundabout and turn → again onto Hammond Way. Follow the road around to the ← to the car park.

# Route 14
*Fool Hardy (Dorset)*

| | |
|---|---|
| **Start/Finish** | Top O'Town car park, Dorchester ST 688 907 |
| **Distance** | 98.5km (61¼ miles) |
| **Ascent** | 1235m (4050ft) |
| **Grade** | |
| **Time** | 4hrs–5hrs 30mins |
| **Feed stations** | The Antelope Inn, Hazelbury Bryan; Abbots, Cerne Abbas; Café 64, Maiden Newton |
| **Access** | The Top O' Town car park can be easily found by following the brown leisure signs for the Military Museum, close to the roundabout at the top of the High Street in Dorchester. |

Fool Hardy is a return ticket to explore the very best of Thomas Hardy's Dorset. He may not have strayed too far from his Dorchester home, but Hardy was a keen cyclist and knocked about with a certain TE Lawrence for a while. He certainly didn't experience Dorset the way we can on our lightweight carbon steeds, but the countryside is still pretty much as it was when he explored it. From the gentle opening miles across dusty heaths and farm lands, Fool Hardy soon builds into a real sportive challenge that covers some pretty tough terrain. But, just like one of Hardy's novels, this route is a roller coaster of highs and lows that takes you right into the heart of his beloved Dorset.

## Overview

Valley floors and quiet country lanes provide a gentle warm-up from Dorchester out to Bere Regis. The pace of life may be slow, but the climb up through Milton Abbas is often foolishly underrated and might require a rest-stop halfway up. A major highlight of the route is the view across the Blackmoor Vale from the summit of Bulbarrow Hill, but don't let this detract you from the superb descent that follows. As tight contours give way to rambling countryside around Hazelbury Bryan, dramatic scenery bounces back with a vengeance as you rapidly descend into Cerne Abbas and claw your way back to the finish line.

**1** Exit ← from the car park in **Dorchester**, descend through the High Street and continue to the roundabout on the **A35**. Go ↑ towards **Tincleton** to reach the crossroads with the **B3390**.

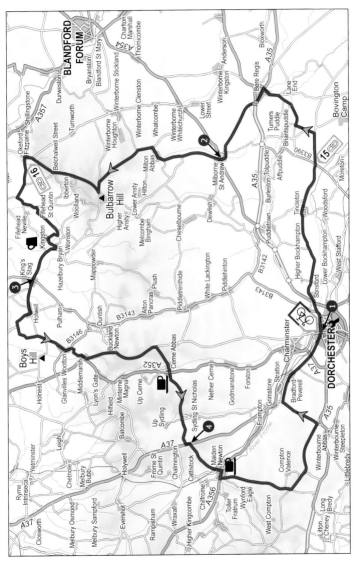

### Link to Route 15
Turn ➡ on the B3390 and take the next turning ⬅ towards **Moreton** to link to Jurassic Classic.

Go ⬆ into the woods, turn ⬅ at the first junction across Throop Heath and continue to a T-junction. Turn ➡, follow the road to another T-junction and turn ⬅ towards Bere Regis. Turn ⬅ next to the Royal Oak pub into **Bere Regis** and go through the village and under the A35 to the crossroads at **Milborne St Andrew**. Go ⬆ at the crossroads to the **A354** and turn ⬅ then immediately ➡ towards Milton Abbas.

**2** Carry on up through **Milton Abbas** to a T-junction and turn ⬅. At the sharp ↱ bend, turn ⬅ to go straight on towards Bulbarrow. At the next T-junction turn ⬅, and then turn ➡ at the summit of **Bulbarrow Hill** to descend to **Belchalwell Street** and Okeford Fitzpaine.

### Link to Route 16
Go straight on past the Royal Oak in **Okeford Fitzpaine** to join Thrill of the Chase for an epic day in the saddle.

Turn ⬅ just before the Royal Oak pub in **Okeford Fitzpaine** towards Fifehead Neville. Continue to a three-way junction and turn ⬅ towards The Fifeheads and Hazelbury Bryan. As you come level with the stream in **Fifehead St Quintin**, turn ➡ over the stream and continue to a T-junction in **Kingston**. Turn ⬅ into

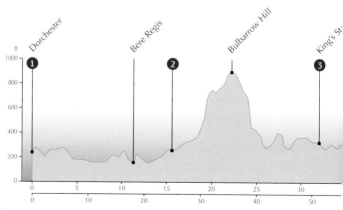

**Throop Heath: Thomas Hardy's back garden**

**Hazelbury Bryan** and turn ➜ just after the Antelope Inn to the crossroads on the **B3143** in **King's Stag**.

**3** Go ↑ at the crossroads to **Holwell** and turn ← at the end of the village for Boys Hill and Glanvilles Wootton. At the T-junction with the **B3146**

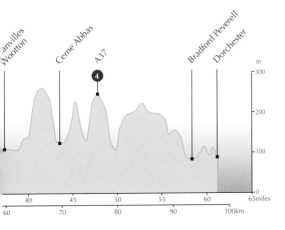

Turn right at the ford and climb to the A37

turn ←, then turn → onto Kennels Lane towards Tiley and continue to a T-junction. Turn ←, follow the road to the Cerne Abbas junction and turn → to descend into **Cerne Abbas**. At the junction beside Abbots café, turn → onto Duck Street to reach the Cerne Abbas Giant car park and continue on to the T-junction with the **A352**. Turn ← to a crossroads and turn → towards Sydling St Nicholas. After descending to a ford, turn → and climb to the **A37**.

**4** Turn ← then immediately → to descend to the T-junction with the **A356** in **Maiden Newton**, and turn →. At the end of the village, turn ← towards Wynford Eagle and West Compton. Climb the steep hill, following the old Roman Road to a crossroads high above Winterbourne Abbas. Turn ←, descend to a crossroads at the bottom of the descent and turn → towards **Bradford Peverell**. Continue over the **A37** into **Dorchester** and climb to a road junction, then turn ← and ← again to return to the car park.

# Route 15
*Jurassic Classic (Dorset)*

| | |
|---|---|
| **Start/Finish** | Sandbanks Ferry Terminal, Poole SZ 036 871 |
| **Distance** | 89.5km (55½ miles) |
| **Ascent** | 870m (2855ft) |
| **Grade** | ▲▲ |
| **Time** | 3hrs 30mins–5hrs |
| **Feed stations** | Moreton Tea Rooms, Moreton; Model Village Café, Corfe Castle (just left of the monument in the village square) |
| **Access** | Exit the A35 at Poole, following the brown leisure signs for Beaches. Continue to the large car park at Sandbanks, at the end of Poole Harbour, then follow the one-way road to the ferry terminal. You may also find free on-street parking among the streets of Sandbanks, just beyond the ferry terminal. |

The anticipation of this ride builds up way before you even disembark from the ferry, as the wonderful anomaly that is the Isle of Purbeck is seen sitting high above the Dorset coastline, like a dormant dragon waiting to play. Sandbanks Ferry unloads its cargo of cyclists onto a perfectly laid-out ribbon of road that leads into flawless sportive training terrain. Flat heathlands and shallow river plains warm the route before that playful dragon wakes with a vengeance at West Lulworth. The hilltops provide stunning views on clear days, and their slopes offer ample descents on which to recover. This truly is the classic sportive playground for cyclists.

Note: this route goes through live army firing ranges after West Lulworth. Although they are open during most weekends and holiday periods, it's worth checking for closure dates (www.dorsetforyou.com/356624). Don't worry, there's a lovely alternative route should the tanks be firing.

## Overview

From Sandbanks Ferry Terminal, the route roller-coasters out to Corfe Castle but the heathland road towards Wareham and beyond provides classic cadence training. The contours soon make a dramatic return as you sweep down into West Lulworth and the arching ridgeline of the Jurassic coast comes into view. The ridgeline rises and falls, and includes a punishing climb in the shape of Whiteway Hill. The final climb out of Swanage leaves tired legs ready for the return ferry.

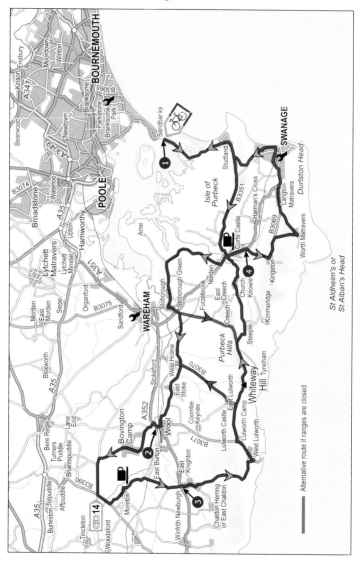

Alternative route if ranges are closed

**Crossing the River Frome at Wool**

**1** Exit the ferry terminal, climb up the **B3351** through **Studland** to the T-junction in front of **Corfe Castle** and turn →. Continue to a large roundabout, turn → towards the railway station and then turn ← towards Arne. Follow the road across Hartland Moor to a small triangular junction and turn ← for Stoborough. Turn ← at the T-junction with the **B3075** in **Stoborough**, and then turn → to the **A351**. Turn ← then immediately →. At the road junction opposite the Springfield Country Hotel, turn → and continue to a crossroads on the **B3070**. Go ↑ to follow the road to the T-junction on the **B3071** in **Wool**. Turn →, then → again over the railway line, then immediately ← over the bridge across the River Frome.

**2** Turn ← onto the road, then ← again into **Bovington Camp**. Follow the road up through Bovington Camp to the crossroads at Clouds Hill (Lawrence of Arabia's old cottage) and turn ←.

Turn left in West Lulworth

## Link to Route 14
To link Jurassic Classic to Fool Hardy, turn → at the next road junction across Throop Heath.

Continue to the crossroads with the **B3390** and turn ←. Go across the River Frome, turn ← to the T-junction in **Moreton** and turn ←. After a cuppa at the tea rooms, turn → to go past a small cemetery (where Lawrence of Arabia is buried) to a small road junction and turn → to climb up onto Winfrith Heath. Continue

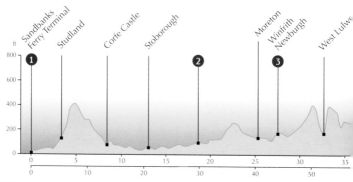

to the **A352** and turn ➡ then immediately ⬅ at the Red Lion pub into **Winfrith Newburgh**.

 Follow the road into **West Lulworth** and turn ⬅ onto West Street just before the church. At the T-junction, turn ⬅ and climb to the road junction beside the army camp. Turn ➡ towards Lulworth Castle.

## Alternative route
Go past the castle entrance and follow the **B3070** to the crossroads at **West Holme**. Turn ➡, continue to the T-junction beside the Springfield Country Hotel and turn ➡. Follow the road through **Creech** and climb to a viewpoint, rejoining the main route at the flagpole beside the sharp ⬅ corner.

Turn ➡ just beyond the castle entrance, and turn ➡ again at a flagpole to climb **Whiteway Hill**. At the summit of the climb turn ➡ to descend towards Church Knowle, and continue to the T-junction beside **Corfe Castle**. Turn ➡, climb up through the village to the road junction for Kingston and turn ➡.

 Just beyond the summit of the climb through **Kingston**, turn ➡ for **Worth Matravers** and continue to the Square and Compass pub. Turn ⬅ at the pub, continue to a T-junction and turn ➡ to descend through **Langton Matravers** to another T-junction. Turn ➡, follow the **A351** to the seafront in **Swanage** and turn ⬅. After the promenade, continue out of Swanage and climb to a T-junction. Turn ➡ and descend through **Studland** to retrace your tyre tracks back to the ferry.

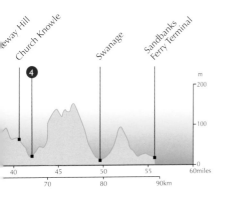

# Route 16
## *Thrill of the Chase (Dorset)*

| | |
|---|---|
| **Start/Finish** | Queen Elizabeth Leisure Centre, Wimborne Minster ST 998 006 |
| **Distance** | 89.75km (55¾ miles) |
| **Ascent** | 785m (2575ft) |
| **Grade** | |
| **Time** | 3hrs 30mins–5hrs |
| **Feed stations** | The Gorge Café, Blandford Forum; The Salt Cellar, Shaftesbury (underneath the town hall) |
| **Access** | From the A31, head into the centre of Wimborne Minster and follow the B3082 (Blandford Forum Road) to the traffic lights at the top of the hill. Just beyond them, turn L into the leisure centre car park. |

Conveniently situated on the northern edge of Bournemouth and Poole, Wimborne Minster is the ideal gateway to the chalk plateau of Cranborne Chase – and what a ride around it this is: a long warm-up, stunning countryside around every corner, easy to follow navigation, and a couple of hills that'll make you wish you were somewhere else! But all roads lead to Shaftesbury as far as this route is concerned, and the journey there is a memorable one, as the climb up into the town leaves an indelible mark on every rider who completes it. Thankfully, after Zig Zag Hill it's pretty much downhill all the way home to Wimborne Minster.

## Overview

The Stour Valley is picturesque and warms the muscles before the hills beyond Blandford Forum kick in, then road leading to Shaftesbury from Okeford Fitzpaine is like the calm before the storm as the cobbled slopes of ancient Shaftesbury demand your full attention. Zig Zag Hill poses little threat if ridden steadily but the return ride through the Tarrant Valley is like riding in overdrive as the miles are simply eaten up. The sharp turn up The Cliff beyond Tarrant Launceston is child's play as the final run into Wimborne Minster allows nothing but a gentle warm-down to soothe aching legs.

 Turn ← out of the car park in **Wimborne Minster** and turn ← towards Pamphill. Go straight past the church, descend to a T-junction at

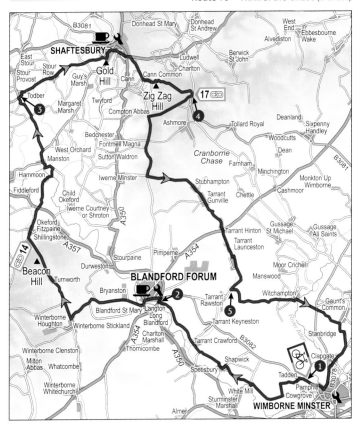

**Cowgrove** and turn ➜ to follow the road along the Stour Valley to the T-junction beside **White Mill**. Turn ➜ towards Shapwick, continue to a small triangular road junction in **Shapwick** with a memorial in the middle and turn ➜. Continue along the Stour Valley to just a few metres before the **A350** at **Blandford Forum**, turn ⬅ onto the cyclepath and go under the bridge.

**2** Turn ⬅ when rejoining the road and continue to the traffic lights. Turn ⬅ again onto East Street (The Gorge Café is on your left, opposite the church) and continue onto West Street to cross over the River Stour. Just after the Bryanston School gates, turn ➡ onto New Road. Follow the road to a T-junction and turn ➡ to descend to the road junction in **Winterborne Stickland**. Turn ➡ and continue through **Turnworth** and up and over **Beacon Hill**. At the T-junction at the bottom of the hill, turn ➡ into **Okeford Fitzpaine**.

## Link to Route 14
Turn ⬅ at the Royal Oak pub in **Okeford Fitzpaine** to join Fool Hardy.

Carry on through the village to the crossroads on the **A357** and go ⬆. Just after crossing the River Stour beyond **Hammoon**, turn ⬅ and continue to the T-junction on the B3091 at **Manston**. Turn ➡ and then ⬅ towards Marnhull and Todber to reach a T-junction on the B3092. Turn ➡, and then turn ➡ again for Stour Row.

**3** Follow the road through **Stour Row** to a large grassy triangle and turn ➡ (ignore the sign to the left for Shaftesbury) to climb to the church of St James in **Shaftesbury**. Go ⬆ onto St James's Street to the bottom of **Gold Hill** and turn ⬅ to climb the cobbles to the Salt Cellar café. Carry on up past the ⬅ side of the café and turn ➡ onto the High Street. Follow the road to a large roundabout and take the second exit onto the **A30** towards Salisbury. Turn immediately ➡ towards Cann Common and turn ➡ at the car garage to climb **Zig Zag Hill**.

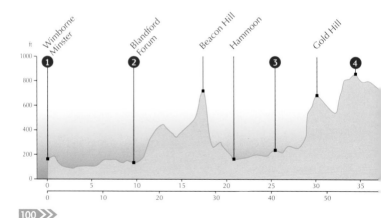

Stay in the Stour Valley and turn right towards Blandford

## Link to Route 17

At the road junction beyond Zig Zag Hill, turn ← and descend sharply towards the Donheads to join Zig Zag.

**4** At the road junction beyond Zig Zag Hill, turn → towards Blandford. Go past the airfield (which has a great café, if you need it) and turn ←, and then turn ← again towards Blandford. Continue to the second cross-roads and turn ← towards **Tarrant Gunville**. Continue through the

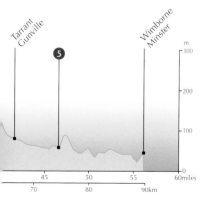

Turn left after Compton Abbas Airfield

Tarrant Valley to the T-junction on the **A354**. Turn ➡ then immediately ⬅ towards **Tarrant Launceston**. Go past the ford, continue towards **Tarrant Rawston** and turn sharp ⬅ up The Cliff towards Witchampton.

**5** Turn ➡ in **Witchampton** and continue to the crossroads on the **B3078**. Go ⬆, continue to a T-junction and turn ➡. Follow the road to the T-junction on the B3078 and turn ⬅ to the traffic lights in **Wimborne Minster**. Turn ➡ and climb to another set of lights. Turn ➡ again and follow the road back to the car park on your left.

# Route 17
*Zig Zag (Wiltshire and Dorset)*

| | |
|---|---|
| **Start/Finish** | Five Rivers Leisure Centre, Salisbury ST 138 302 |
| **Distance** | 104.5km (65½ miles) |
| **Ascent** | 1235m (4050ft) |
| **Grade** |  |
| **Time** | 4hrs–5hrs 30mins |
| **Feed stations** | Five Rivers Leisure centre café, Salisbury; Beatons Tearooms, Tisbury; The Salt Cellar, Shaftesbury (underneath the town hall); Costa Coffee, Shaftesbury |
| **Access** | The leisure centre can be found off the ring road in Salisbury just off the A345 on the Old Sarum Road, where it is well signposted by brown tourist signs. |

If you don't like climbing hills, look away now. But if you do turn to another route, you're sure to miss out on one of the finest sportives in all of south west England. The countryside is stunning; navigation is a doddle; feed stations are plentiful and the terrain is an excellent pre-event test of fitness and determination. Zig Zag Hill may be famous – or, indeed, infamous – but it's not the most challenging climb here (just wait till you leave the A30 and turn left for Alvediston). Zig Zag is festooned with high ridge lines and deep valley floors, along with a series of hills that will pay handsome dividends, should you be training hard for a sportive event.

## Overview
Heading out of Salisbury along the Avon Valley is a picture of serenity, but that's all kissed goodbye as soon as you start to climb out of Middle Woodford. A long, challenging climb out of the Wylye Valley leads to Dinton and beyond to Tisbury, before Shaftesbury raises its head following another tough climb from Motcombe. The reward is an excellent selection of cafés in the town centre. Beyond Zig Zag Hill, the flowing route after Donhead St Andrew and Ansty is abruptly ground to a snail's pace by a wicked 20° climb over the escarpment to Alvediston. The Chalke Valley floor gently winds its way back towards the route's last two climbs, before the descent of Snake Hill finishes off a superb ride.

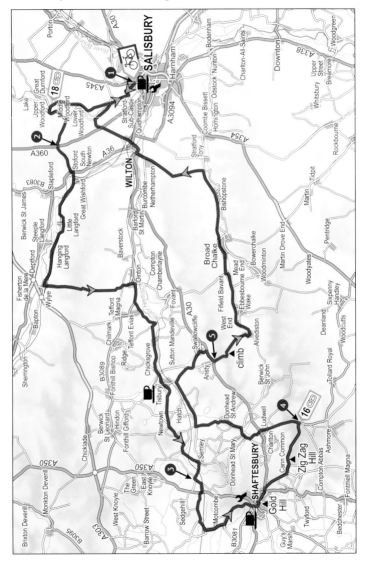

Prime Wiltshire tarmac towards Tisbury

**1** Just before exiting the leisure centre car park in **Salisbury**, turn ←
onto the cyclepath, go past the running track and follow the cyclepath
alongside houses to the road junction in **Stratford-Sub-Castle**. Turn ←
to go through the village to the bridge, and turn → then immediately
← to follow the road to a T-junction beside the River Avon at **Upper
Woodford**.

## Link to Route 18
To extend this route, turn → at **Upper Woodford** and join Plain Sailing.

Turn ← into **Middle Woodford**, turn → opposite the red phone box and climb to
the crossroads with the **A360**.

**2** Go ↑ to descend to the **A36** at **Stoford**. Turn ← then immediately →
into **Great Wishford**. Turn → at the Royal Oak pub and follow the road
towards Wylye. At the road junction with the railway lights in **Wylye**
turn ← to climb towards Dinton. At the crossroads in **Dinton** turn →
onto the **B3089**, then continue to a road junction beside a thatched
cottage and turn ← towards Tisbury. After entering **Tisbury** turn ←
opposite a series of old cottages onto The Avenue and continue to a
T-junction in the village square opposite Beatons Tearooms. Turn ←
then immediately → onto Church Street to climb through **Newtown**
and into Semley. At the T-junction in **Semley** turn →, then go under the
old railway line and turn ← opposite some new barns onto Station Road
towards Shaftesbury.

Beyond Zig Zag Hill turn left towards the Donheads

**3** Continue to the **A350** and turn → then immediately ← towards the village of Motcombe. At the mini roundabout at the far end of **Motcombe**
turn ← and climb towards Shaftesbury. At the T-junction with the
**B3081** turn ← to go under the flyover and carefully turn → onto New
Road and into **Shaftesbury**. At the T-junction at the top turn → and
follow the road past the town hall and along the High Street to a large

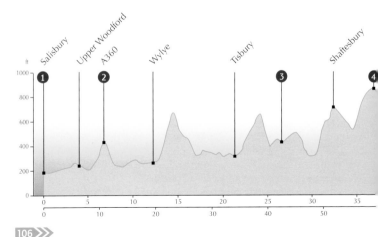

roundabout. Take the second exit onto the **A30** and then turn immediately ➡ towards Cann Common. Turn ⬅ at the car garage and climb **Zig Zag Hill**.

## Link to Route 16
At the road junction beyond Zig Zag Hill, turn ➡ and follow signs for Blandford Forum to join Thrill of the Chase.

**4** At the road junction beyond Zig Zag Hill turn ⬅ towards the Donheads and descend to the junction with the **A30**. Go ⬆ onto a narrow lane to a T-junction, and turn ➡. Continue to the next junction and turn ➡ for Donhead St Andrew. At the next T-junction turn ⬅ and continue through **Donhead St Andrew**. Follow this road towards Tisbury to a T-junction and turn ➡ for Swallowcliffe. On reaching the A30 in **Swallowcliffe**, turn ➡, continue to a hollow in the road and turn sharp ⬅ for Alvediston.

**5** At the T-junction in **Alvediston** turn ⬅ to follow the Chalke Valley floor through **Broad Chalke** to **Bishopstone**, and turn ⬅ uphill towards Wilton. At the traffic lights in **Wilton** turn ➡ to the roundabout on the **A36** and go ⬆ up the long hill to the **A360**. Go ⬆ and descend Snake Hill to the T-junction in the Woodford Valley and turn ➡. Cross the river into Stratford-Sub-Castle and turn ➡ at the sharp ↰ corner onto the original cyclepath to return to the leisure centre in **Salisbury**.

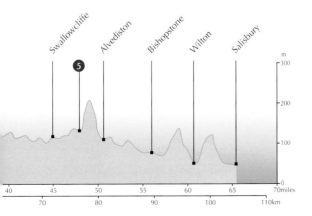

# Route 18
*Plain Sailing (Wiltshire)*

| | |
|---|---|
| **Start/Finish** | Five Rivers Leisure Centre, Salisbury ST 138 302 |
| **Distance** | 70km (43½ miles) |
| **Ascent** | 575m (1885ft) |
| **Grade** | ▲ |
| **Time** | 2hrs 30mins–3hrs 30mins |
| **Feed stations** | Five Rivers Leisure Centre café, Salisbury; The Plume of Feathers, Shrewton; The Barford Inn, Barford St Martin |
| **Access** | The leisure centre can be found off the ring road in Salisbury just off the A345 on the Old Sarum Road, where it is well signposted by brown tourist signs. |

The placid roads along the Woodford Valley kick off this short training loop that is also perfectly placed to act as an add-on to the neighbouring Zig Zag. But Plain Sailing works just as well as a stand-alone ride for beginners or intermediates looking to test themselves for a 50-mile event. Not without its fair share of excellent climbs, the route also provides plenty of flat ground on which to work on your cadence, and to recover before climbing again. Plain Sailing is a beautifully presented small package that delivers on all fronts.

## Overview
With an absence of any real climbs for the majority of its length, this ride is all about speed and cadence. After getting the wheels rolling out of Salisbury and along the Woodford Valley, the roads beyond the garrison town of Larkhill are

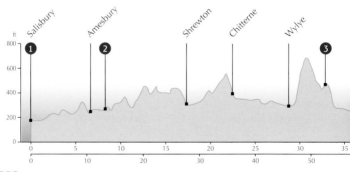

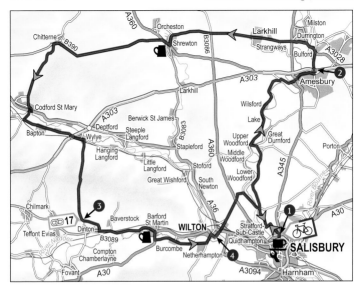

normally light on traffic (aside from the odd tank or two); this makes them the perfect location for an all-out time trial or interval session training ride. After turning into the Wylye Valley at Codford St Mary, the rolling landscape is soon substituted by the challenging climb towards Dinton. After the long climb from Wilton slows proceedings, the sweeping bends of Snake Hill swiftly return riders into the Woodford Valley and the finish line.

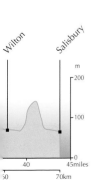

**1** Just before exiting the leisure centre car park in **Salisbury**, turn ← onto the cyclepath, go past the running track and follow the cyclepath alongside houses to the road junction in **Stratford-Sub-Castle**. Turn ← to go through the village to the bridge, and turn → then immediately ← to follow the road to a T-junction beside the River Avon at **Upper Woodford**. Turn → and continue to a T-junction. Turn → into **Amesbury**, go ↑ at the traffic lights and continue onto London Road. At the second (large) roundabout turn ← over the **A303** towards Durrington.

**2** At the T-junction with the **A3028** turn ← to a roundabout and go ↑ through **Larkhill** to the roundabout in **Shrewton**. Turn → to pass the old town gaol then take the next ← onto the **B390**, signposted Chitterne. Near the end of **Chitterne** turn ← just before the Kings Head pub towards Codford St Mary. At the T-junction in **Codford St Mary** turn ← towards Salisbury to the T-junction with the **A36** and turn → then immediately ← towards Sherrington. Continue to

Shrewton: don't go straight to gaol, turn right

a T-junction and turn ← towards Wylye. After going under the **A303** in **Wylye**, turn → onto Teapot Street and then turn → again onto Fore Street. Continue to the road junction with the railway traffic lights at the end of the village and turn → towards Dinton.

**3** Continue to the very narrow road junction atop the summit of the second steep climb (beside the Dinton signpost).

## Link to Route 17
Go SA at the narrow road junction into Dinton to join Zig Zag.

Turn ← at the narrow road junction and follow the narrow lane to a T-junction with the **B3089**. Turn ← to the T-junction with the **A30** in **Barford St Martin**. Turn →, go over the river and turn ← towards Wilton. Continue to a T-junction, turn ← to the traffic lights in the centre of **Wilton** and turn →.

**4** Continue to the roundabout on the **A36** and go ↑ to climb to the **A360**. Go ↑, descend Snake Hill to the T-junction in the Woodford Valley and turn →. Follow the road into **Stratford-Sub-Castle**, turn → at the sharp ↰ corner onto the cyclepath and continue to the leisure centre in **Salisbury**.

# Route 19
## *Cheval Blanc (Wiltshire)*

| | |
|---|---|
| **Start/Finish** | Lime Kiln Leisure Centre, Royal Wootton Bassett SU 069 830 |
| **Distance** | 68km (42¼ miles) |
| **Ascent** | 595m (1950ft) |
| **Grade** | ▲ |
| **Time** | 2hrs 30mins–3hrs 30mins |
| **Feed stations** | Caffé Nero, Marlborough; The Bridge Inn, near Horton |
| **Access** | Exit the M4 at Junction 16 and follow the A3102 into Royal Wootton Bassett. At the road junction just before a petrol station, turn R into Lime Kiln and continue to a mini roundabout. Turn R and the leisure centre will be found on your left. |

With no fewer than four white horses dominating the chalk escarpment, you can tell you're in Marlborough Country here. There's nothing too challenging about the hills on Cheval Blanc – short and sharp or long and gentle, the beautifully surfaced climbs take precedence without hurting the mind or body too much. Quiet country lanes and short stretches of smooth major roads provide an easy route that's both enjoyable and picturesque. Whether you intend to plod along or time trial it, Cheval Blanc provides an ideal test bed on which to prove your worth.

## Overview

The slick tarmac road that feeds the chalk downs from Royal Wootton Bassett through Broad Town and Broad Hinton offers low resistance and a great chance for riders to attack the route's first two short climbs with confidence. Beyond Marlborough the quiet, almost traffic-free roads through Alton Barnes and Bishops Cannings cut through some stunning countryside. And, with only the small hiccup of the A4 to slow your pace, you soon return to quiet, well surfaced country lanes and horse-laden hillsides.

**1** Turn ➡ out of the car park in **Royal Wootton Basset**, return to the High Street and turn ➡. Continue to the junction just before the old market building and turn ⬅ onto Station Road towards Broad Hinton and Broad Town. At the mini roundabout go ⬆ to follow the road out

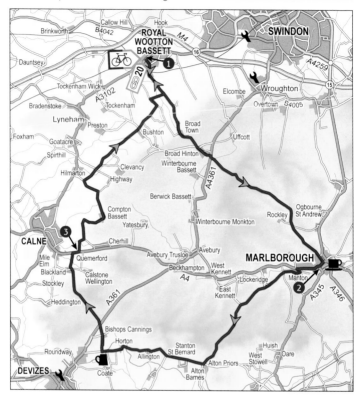

through **Broad Hinton** and reach the crossroads on the **A4361**. Go ↑ towards Marlborough. At the T-junction on the edge of **Marlborough** turn ➡ to descend to the High Street (reputedly the second widest high street in Britain). Turn ➡ to a mini roundabout at the end of the High Street and turn ➡ to follow the **A4**.

**2** Continue along the A4 for 500m then turn ⬅ onto a narrow lane beside the building called East Lodge. Follow the gravelly lane to a small T-junction and turn ➡ to the T-junction in **Manton**. Turn ⬅ to continue towards Lockeridge. At a grassy triangular road junction turn ⬅ towards Woodborough and Alton Barnes. Climb through the gap in the

On exiting Marlborough turn left at East Lodge

EAST
LODGE

chalk escarpment and descend into **Alton Priors**. Turn → opposite the white horse (behind your right shoulder) towards Devizes. Follow the road to the Bridge Inn beyond **Horton** and then turn → towards the village of Bishops Cannings. Continue through **Bishops Cannings** to the **A361** and, at the awkward junction, carefully go ↑ towards Calne. Continue to the A4 and turn → then immediately ← towards the village of Compton Bassett.

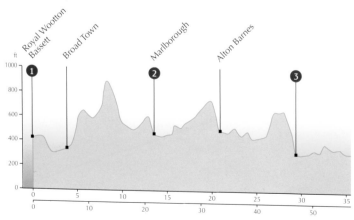

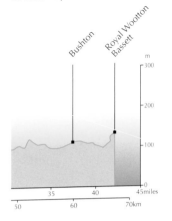

**3** Continue through **Compton Bassett** to a road junction and turn ➡ towards Bushton and Royal Wootton Bassett (blue cycle route). Continue past **Bushton** to a T-junction and turn ⬅ into **Royal Wootton Bassett**. At the mini roundabout at Station Road turn ⬅ to climb to the High Street. Turn ➡, continue to the traffic lights beside the petrol station and turn ⬅ onto Lime Kiln to return to the car park.

## Link to Route 20

If you have the legs for it, ignore the turning onto Lime Kiln and continue ⬆. Pass through **Hook** and head towards Purton, where you can harness up with Clyffe Hanger. Be warned, however: linked together, these two thoroughbreds are tougher than they look.

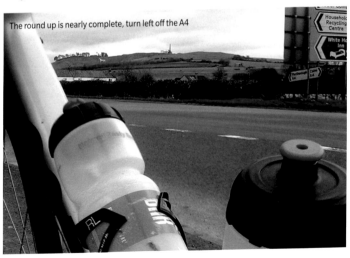

The round up is nearly complete, turn left off the A4

# Route 20
## *Clyffe Hanger (Wiltshire)*

| | |
|---|---|
| **Start/Finish** | Lime Kiln Leisure Centre, Royal Wootton Bassett SU 069 830 |
| **Distance** | 104km (64¾ miles) |
| **Ascent** | 635m (2085ft) |
| **Grade** | ▲▲ |
| **Time** | 3hrs 30mins–5hrs |
| **Feed stations** | Eliot Arms, South Cerney; The Wheatsheaf Inn, Oaksey |
| **Access** | Exit the M4 at Junction 16 and follow the A3102 into Royal Wootton Bassett. At the road junction just before a petrol station, turn R into Lime Kiln and continue to a mini roundabout. Turn R and the leisure centre will be found on your left. |

This fun but challenging route plays out like an old Alfred Hitchcock thriller. At the beginning you (the good guy) spend a great deal of time wondering where the contours (the bad guys) are. But the further into the ride you go and the more the story unfolds, the lumpier and more intriguing the route becomes. You might also fail to notice how tired you're getting until it's too late. Then right at the end, when you think you can't possibly go on, the exciting climax kicks in and the final hill climb (defeating the last of the bad guys) is a real Clyffe Hanging finale. As the end credits roll, it's just a simple ride back to the finish line in time for tea and medals.

## Overview
Purton, Minety, Ashton Keynes and South Cerney all work as key markers on the nearly contour-free opening gambit. While Ewen, Kemble and Tarlton start to collect ups and downs, there's still nothing more than enjoyable rolling countryside stretched out before you. The section of road between the A433 and A429 offers up time-trialling heaven before the contours squeeze up tightly after crossing the M4. The final climactic climb up through Clyffe Pypard sets riders up for a superb downhill stretch before returning to the finish line at Royal Wootton Bassett.

**1** Exit ➡ from the car park in **Royal Wootton Bassett** and return to the High Street. Turn ➡, continue to a roundabout and go ⬆, over the **M4**, to the mini roundabout in **Purton**. Turn ⬅, continue to the crossroads with the **B4696** and go ⬆. Follow the road to the crossroads in **Minety**

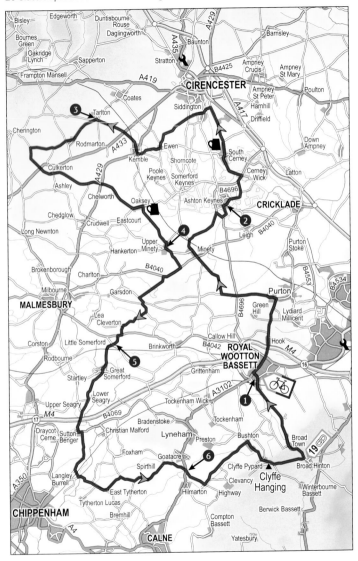

Turn left towards Siddington

and go ⬆. After going around a sharp ⬅ bend, turn ➡ onto Sawyers Hill, go under the railway bridge and turn ➡ towards Ashton Keynes. Follow the road as it narrows to the T-junction on the B4696. Turn ➡, and then turn ⬅ towards Ashton Keynes. Continue to a small cross-roads in **Ashton Keynes** and turn ➡ onto Happy Land.

**2** Just beyond Happy Land, turn ⬅ onto Rixon Gate and continue to the **B4696**. Turn ➡, then turn ⬅ onto Broadway Lane and continue to the T-junction on the High Street in **South Cerney**. Turn ➡ then imme-diately ⬅ onto Clarks Hay. Continue to a road junction and turn ⬅ onto South Cerney Road to follow NCN Route 45 towards Siddington. Continue to a T-junction and turn ⬅, then turn ➡ opposite the post office in **Siddington** onto Park Way. Continue to a T-junction and turn ⬅ then immediately ➡ towards Ewen. At the T-junction in **Ewen** turn ➡ and continue to the staggered crossroads in **Kemble**. Go ⬆ to the **A429** and turn ➡ then immediately ⬅ onto Windmill Road towards Tarlton and the A433. Go ⬆ at the **A433** and climb towards Tarlton.

**3** Continue through **Tarlton** and go past a large water tower to continue along the lane towards Rodmarton. Go ⬆ at the staggered crossroads in **Rodmarton** to continue to a large triangular grass road junction. Turn ➡ towards Cherington then, after a 1.5km straight section of road, turn ⬅ at the road junction in the woods and continue to the A433. Go ⬆

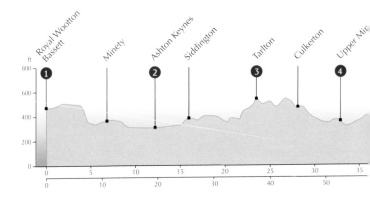

at the main road, through Culkerton and continue to the **A429**. Go ↑
to follow the road into Oaksey. Turn → at the church in **Oaksey** onto
Minety Lane and continue to the T-junction in **Upper Minety**.

**4** Turn ← at the T-junction, then turn → onto Dog Trap Lane and continue
to the T-junction with the **B4040**. Turn → for 1.3km and then turn ←
(possibly not signposted). Continue past a large water tower and a lake
to a T-junction and turn ←. Continue for 400m to a small red postbox

Keep your eyes peeled for Brinkworth

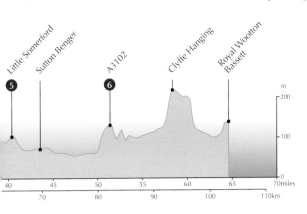

and turn → towards Brinkworth. Go past the first road junction and then turn → at the next junction (possibly not signposted) to follow the lane to a T-junction on the **B4042**. Turn → to the next junction then turn ← towards the Somerfords.

**5** At the T-junction in **Little Somerford** turn → and follow the road through **Great Somerford** to continue over the **M4** to the T-junction with the **B4069** at **Sutton Benger**. Turn ← then immediately → towards Langley Burrell. Continue to a small road junction and turn ← towards East Tytherton and Calne. Continue under the railway line to a T-junction and turn ← towards Bremhill, Tytherton and Calne. Follow the road through **East Tytherton** to a T-junction and turn → to climb up to another T-junction. Turn ← and follow the lane to the **A3102**.

**6** Go ↑ at the staggered crossroads on the **A3102**, continue to a T-junction and then turn ← towards Bushton. At the crossroads beside the dorma bungalows in **Bushton**, turn → towards Clyffe Pypard and Broad Hinton, then climb sharply up **Clyffe Hanging** to a T-junction near **Broad Hinton**.

## Link to Route 19
Turn → at **Broad Hinton** to hoof it around Cheval Blanc for more pain.

Turn ← and follow the road into **Royal Wootton Bassett** to a mini roundabout. Turn ← to climb to the High Street, and turn → onto it. Continue to a petrol station and turn ← onto Lime Kiln to return to the leisure centre.

# Appendix A
*Bike shops and cycle repair outfits*

**Route 1**
Bodmin Bikes
3 Hamley Court
Dennison Road
Bodmin
Cornwall PL31 2LL
Tel: 01208 73192
sales@bodminbikes.co.uk
www.bodminbikes.co.uk

**Route 2**
Rockin Bikes
Unit 7 & 8
Harrowbeer Mews
Leg O'mutton
Yelverton
Devon PL20 6AD
Tel: 01822 258022
help@rockinbikes.co.uk
www.rockinbikes.co.uk

Bigpeaks.com
Unit C1 Linhay Business Park
Ashburton
Devon TQ13 7UP
Tel: 01364 654080
info@bigpeaks.com
www.bigpeaks.com

**Route 3**
Haldon Forest Cycle Hire
Haldon Forest Park
Bullers Hill
Kennford
Exeter
Devon EX6 7XR
Tel: 01392 833768
info@forestcyclehire.co.uk
www.forestcyclehire.co.uk

**Route 4**
The Bike Shop
30 Leat Street
Tiverton
Devon EX16 5LG
Tel: 01884 253979

**Route 5**
Exmoor Cycles
6 Parkhouse Road
Minehead
Somerset TA24 8AB
Tel: 01643 705307
sales@exmoorcycles.co.uk
www.exmoorcycles.co.uk

**Route 6**
Cycle1 King Street
Honiton
Devon EX14 1AB
Tel: 01404 47211
sales@cycle1.co.uk
www.cycle1.co.uk

**Routes 6–7**
Ralph Colman Cycles
69–71 Station Road
Taunton
Somerset TA1 1PA
Tel: 01823 275822
ralphcolman@bike-uk.co.uk

**Route 7**
King's Cycles
7 Cornhill
Wellington
Somerset TA21 8LU
Tel: 01823 662260
info@kingscycles.co.uk
www.kingscycles.co.uk

**Route 8**
The Bicycle Chain
13–15 Locking Road
Weston-super-Mare
Somerset BS23 3BY
Tel: 01934 629370
info@bicyclechain.co.uk
www.bicyclechain.co.uk

**Route 9**
Bike City
8 Queen Street
Wells
Somerset BA5 2DP
Tel: 01749 670002
bikecityltd@live.co.uk
www.bikecity.biz

Live2Ride
The Old Courthouse
Waterloo
Frome
Somerset BA11 3FE
Tel: 01373 469590
www.live2ride.co.uk

**Route 10**
Evans Cycles
Lewins Mead
Bristol BS1 2PY
Tel: 0117 927 7639
www.evanscycles.com/stores/
Bristol

Bad Ass Bikes
Burrington Coombe
Bristol BS40 7AT
Tel: 01761 462011
info@badassbikes.co.uk
www.badassbikes.co.uk

**Route 11**
Blast Bikes
Brick House
21 Horse Street
Chipping Sodbury
BristolBS37 6DA
Tel: 01454 319122
info@blastbikes.co.uk
www.blastbikes.co.uk

### Route 12

559 Bikes
4 Manor Way
Chepstow
Monmouthshire
NP16 5HZ
Tel: 01291 626126
info@559bikes.com
www.559bikes.com

Dean Forest Cycles
New Road
Parkend
Gloucestershire GL15 4HG
Tel: 01594 368009
contactus@deanforestcycles.co.uk
www.deanforestcycles.co.uk

### Routes 13 and 20

Independent Bikeworks
Unit 3 The Exchange
Brewery Court
Cirencester
Gloucestershire GL7 1JL
Tel: 01285 238184
info@independent-works.co.uk
www.independent-works.co.uk

### Route 14

Dorchester Cycles
31 Great Western Road
Dorchester
Dorset DT1 1UF
Tel: 01305 268787
sales@dorchestercycles.co.uk
www.dorchestercycles.co.uk

### Route 15

Ride Bike
111 Commercial Road
Lower Parkstone
Poole
Dorset BH14 0JD
Tel: 01202 741744
shop@ridebike.co.uk
www.ridebike.co.uk

Cycle Experience
Wareham Station
Northport
Wareham
DorsetBH20 4AS
Tel: 01929 556601
wareham@cyclex.co.uk
www.cyclex.co.uk/wareham

Charlie the Bike Monger
5 Queen's Road
Swanage
Dorset
BH19 2EQ
Tel: 01929 475833
bikemonger@yahoo.co.uk
www.charliethebikemonger.com

### Route 16

Samways & Son
70 Leigh Road
Wimborne Minster
Dorset BH21 2AJ
Tel: 01202 882960
info@samwaysandson.co.uk
www.samwaysandson.co.uk

Offcamber
38 Salisbury Street
Blandford Forum
Dorset
Tel: 01258 458677
www.offcamber.co.uk

### Routes 16–17

Hammoon Cycles
Unit 24J Wincombe Business Park
Shaftesbury
Dorset SP7 9QJ
Tel: 01747 850622

### Route 17–18

Stonehenge Cycles
86 Fisherton Street
Salisbury
Wiltshire SP2 7QY
Tel: 01722 334915
sales@stonehengecycles.com
www.stonehengecycles.com

### Route 19

Bikes'N'Boards
Brian Roberts-Phare
Unit 2
121 Southbroom Road
Devizes
Wiltshire SN10 1LY
Tel: 01380 729621
info@bikesnboards.co.uk
www.bikesnboards.co.uk

### Routes 19–20

Hargroves Cycles
Unit 9 Penzance Drive
Churchward Park
Swindon
Wiltshire SN5 7RX
Tel: 01793 528208
swindon@hargrovescycles.co.uk
www.hargrovescycles.co.uk

# Appendix B
*Useful contacts*

## Sportive cycling websites

### British Cycling
www.britishcycling.org.uk, the website of Britain's cycling governing body, is a real mine of sportive information. You'll find a comprehensive events calendar, plus a whole load of training and nutrition tips. The website is simple to navigate, easy to read and features clear instructions on how to enter.

### Cyclosport
The Cyclosport website – www.cyclosport.org – has an excellent 'magazine' look to it. It's not only full of features on sportive events at home and abroad, but also bikes and kit. A really useful website aimed at those riders with a little more experience, due to the continental European element, but an excellent and informative website for the sportive rider nonetheless.

### UKcyclingevents
UKcyclingevents (www.ukcyclingevents.co.uk) is the home of one of the UK's premier sportive event organisers. The website is heavy on sponsorship, but at least you know what you're getting for your money when you sign on and collect your goodie bag.

### RoadcyclingUK.com
Sign up to RoadcyclingUK.com's musette email at www.roadcyclinguk.com and get all the latest reviews, guides and race news from the world of professional, amateur and sportive cycling. RCUK is stylish and informative, with buyer's guides, how tos and in-depth analysis of everything from tyres to training. If you're really into your sport then RCUK is certainly one to sign up for.

### Cycling Weekly
One of the UK's most popular magazines, Cycling Weekly also has a life of its own on the internet, at www.cyclingweekly.co.uk. This website is packed with features on bikes, clothing, kit, components, you name it; great articles on nutrition too. A full events calendar complements the information overload. It is a real one-stop shop for sportive riders.

### Tourist information
For a list of all the tourist information centres in the region as well as details of events, things to do, accommodation options and even great pubs, go to www.visitsouthwest.co.uk.

### Accommodation websites
www.visitdevon.co.uk/accommodation

www.westcountrycottages.co.uk

www.visitcornwall.com/accommodation

www.southwestholidaycottages.com

www.visitwiltshire.co.uk/accommodation

www.cotswolds.com/accommodation

www.visit-dorset.com/accommodation

www.visitsomerset.co.uk/accommodation

www.visitbristol.co.uk/accommodation

www.visitbath.co.uk/accommodation

www.pitchup.com/tents/England/South_West

### Hospitals with A&E facilities
Royal Cornwall Hospital (Treliske)
Treliske
Truro
Cornwall TR1 3LQ
Tel: 01872 250000

Derriford Hospital
Derriford Road
Crownhill
Plymouth
Devon PL6 8DH
Tel: 01752 202082

Royal Devon and Exeter Hospital (Wonford)
Barrack Road
Exeter
Devon EX2 5DW
Tel: 01392 411611

Bristol Royal Infirmary
Marlborough Street
Bristol BS2 8HW
Tel: 0117 923 0000

# Appendix B – Useful contacts

Musgrove Park Hospital
Parkfield Drive
Taunton
Somerset  TA1 5DA
Tel: 01823 333444

Poole Hospital
Longfleet Road
Poole
Dorset  BH15 2JB
Tel: 01202 665511

Salisbury District Hospital
Odstock Road
Salisbury
Wiltshire  SP2 8BJ
Tel: 01722 336262

The Great Western Hospital
Marlborough Road
Swindon
Wiltshire  SN3 6BB
Tel: 01793 604020

Cheltenham General Hospital
Sandford Road
Cheltenham
Gloucestershire  GL53 7AN
Tel: 0300 422 2222

Royal Gwent Hospital
Cardiff Road
Newport  NP20 2UB
Tel: 01633 234234

Weston General Hospital
Grange Road
Uphill
Weston-super-Mare
Somerset  BS23 4TQ
Tel: 01934 636363

Royal United Hospital
Combe Park
Bath
Somerset  BA1 3NG
Tel: 01225 428331

# Listing of Cicerone Guides